# A Question
## of
# Sport
## Quiz Book

# A Question
## of
# Sport
## Quiz Book

1

BBC Books, an imprint of Ebury Publishing
20 Vauxhall Bridge Road,
London SW1V 2SA

BBC Books is part of the Penguin Random House group of companies
whose addresses can be found at global.penguinrandomhouse.com

Penguin
Random House
UK

First published by BBC Books in 2020

www.penguin.co.uk

A CIP catalogue record for this book is available from the British Library

ISBN 9781785945397

Printed and bound in Great Britain by Clays Ltd., Elcograf S.p.A.

Penguin Random House is committed to a sustainable future for
our business, our readers and our planet. This book is made
from Forest Stewardship Council® certified paper.

# Contents

# Game 1

# One-Minute Round

1. Which football team play their home games at The Valley?

2. Can you solve this sporting equation? '91EC for JW in RU'

3. In which sport do the USA and Europe compete for the Mosconi Cup?

4. 'SUCH GLIB COAL' is an anagram of which basketball team?

5. Sue Barker won the French Open singles title in which year?

6. What number comes between three and seven on a standard dartboard?

7. Lydia Ko and Peter Snell have both won Olympic medals for which country?

8. These three sports stars all share parts of their names with things you might associate with Robin Hood...

   Tim **?** (Football)
   Jack **?** (Rugby League)
   Hassan **?** (Boxing)

# Mystery Guest

**In this round you are given three clues
to a sports star's identity.**

## Who is this Mystery Guest?

1. I won individual gold for Great Britain at the 2012 Olympics.

2. I became the WBC International Heavyweight Champion in only my ninth professional fight.

3. In 2019, I suffered my first professional defeat, which I avenged in a rematch later that year in Saudi Arabia.

## Who is this Mystery Guest?

1. I won my first World Championship race in 1992.

2. I won the TV show *I'm a Celebrity… Get Me Out of Here!* in 2014.

3. I won four World Superbike titles with Ducati between 1994 and 1999.

# Home or Away

**In this round there is a choice of a home question
for one point or an away question for two.**

*Do you want a home question on Football for one point or an
away question on Horse Racing for two?*

1.  **Football.** In March 2012, who became the first African player to
    score 100 goals in the Premier League?

2.  **Horse Racing.** Since 1966, which racecourse has hosted the
    Scottish Grand National?

*Do you want a home question on Golf for one point or an away
question on Formula One for two?*

1.  **Golf.** In 2008, which Irishman became only the third golfer in the
    last 25 years to retain the Open Championship?

2.  **Formula One.** Which team, in its only year in Formula One, won
    the 2009 World Championship team with Jenson Button?

*Do you want a home question on Cricket for one point or an away question on Baseball for two?*

1. **Cricket.** Which Indian batsman scored the most runs at the 2019 Cricket World Cup, including a record five hundreds?

2. **Baseball.** Who are the only Major League Baseball team to win the World Series that aren't based in the USA?

*Do you want a home question on Tennis for one point or an away question on Snooker for two?*

1. **Tennis.** Which Romanian won the Women's Singles title at the 2018 French Open, ten years after winning the Girls' Singles title?

2. **Snooker.** Who, in 2010, became the first Australian since Eddie Charlton to reach the final of the World Championship?

# Top Ten

**Name the ten countries at the top
of 2018 Winter Olympic medal table.**

There's a point for each one you correctly identify, but guess one
wrong and you lose your points from this round…

1 ........................................................................

2 ........................................................................

3 ........................................................................

4 ........................................................................

5 ........................................................................

6 ........................................................................

7 ........................................................................

8 ........................................................................

9 ........................................................................

10 ........................................................................

# Buzzer Round

**All the questions in this round are about sports stars bursting onto the scene as youngsters...**

1. Who became World Champion at the age of just 15 when he won 10m platform gold in 2009?

2. Martina Hingis became the youngest Grand Slam Singles Champion of the twentieth century by winning which tournament?

3. In 2016, at the age of 18, who became the youngest winner of a Formula One Grand Prix?

4. Pelé scored twice as a 17-year-old for Brazil in the 1958 World Cup Final against which team?

5. By winning the 1993 UK Championship, which snooker player became the youngest winner of a professional ranking tournament?

6. Swimmer Katie Ledecky won 800m Freestyle Olympic gold as a 15-year-old whilst representing which country?

7. In 2010, who became the youngest Rugby Union player to score a try on debut for Wales?

8. In what year did Tiger Woods become the youngest ever winner of the US Masters?

9. In 1989, which 16-year-old became the youngest cricketer to represent India in Test cricket?

10. In which sport did 15-year-old Tara Lipinsky win Winter Olympic gold?

# Sprint Finish

**Describe these ten sporting words and phrases to your team...**

1. Wasps

2. Boxing ring

3. Carl Lewis

4. Goal difference

5. Podium

6. Captain's armband

7. Martina Navratilova

8. Champions League

9. Bobsleigh

10. Last lap

# **Game 1** Answers

**One-Minute Round**

1. Charlton Athletic; 2. 91 England Caps for Jonny Wilkinson in Rugby Union;
3. Pool; 4. Chicago Bulls; 5. 1976; 6. 19; 7. New Zealand; 8. Tim SHERWOOD,
Jack LITTLEJOHN, Hassan SHERIF

**Mystery Guest**

Anthony Joshua, Carl Fogarty

**Home or Away**

1. Football. Didier Drogba
2. Horse Racing. Ayr

1. Golf. Padraig Harrington
2. Formula One. Brawn

1. Cricket. Rohit Sharma
2. Baseball. Toronto Blue Jays

1. Tennis. Simona Halep
2. Snooker. Neil Robertson

**Top Ten**

Norway
Germany
Canada
USA
Netherlands
Sweden
South Korea
Switzerland
France
Austria

**Buzzer Round**

1. Tom Daley; 2. Australian Open; 3. Max Verstappen; 4. Sweden;
5. Ronnie O'Sullivan; 6. USA; 7. George North; 8. 1997; 9. Sachin Tendulkar;
10. Figure Skating

# Game 2

# One-Minute Round

1. Which Rugby Union team play their home games at Welford Road?

2. Can you solve this sporting equation? '15R and 15B in a MB'

3. In which sport would you see a dig and a spike?

4. 'SEE MILLIONS' is an anagram of which footballer?

5. In which year did Manchester host the Commonwealth Games?

6. What number did Kevin Pietersen wear for England in One Day International cricket?

7. Mario Ančić and Blanka Vlašić have both competed internationally for which country?

8. These three sports stars all share parts of their names with types of flowers…

   Justin **?** (Golf)
   **?** Melhuish (Weightlifting)
   Dennis **?** (Cricket)

# Mystery Guest

**In this round you are given three clues
to a sports star's identity.**

## *Who is this Mystery Guest?*

1.  I started my athletics training aged 12, but would leave it behind to join the British Army.

2.  I was made a Dame in the 2005 New Year's Honours list.

3.  I am an Olympic champion in both the 800m and 1500m.

## *Who is this Mystery Guest?*

1.  I took my first Test wicket in 1992 by dismissing Ravi Shastri.

2.  I played for Hampshire County Cricket Club from 2000 to 2007.

3.  I dismissed Mike Gatting in the 1993 Ashes series with the 'ball of the century'.

# Home or Away

**In this round there is a choice of a home question for one point or an away question for two.**

*Do you want a home question on Rugby Union for one point or an away question on Motor Sport for two?*

1. **Rugby Union.** Which Welsh winger was the top try scorer at the 2019 Rugby World Cup?

2. **Motor Sport.** In 2019, Marc Marquez won his fourth consecutive World title in which motor sport?

*Do you want a home question on Football for one point or an away question on Netball for two?*

1. **Football.** Which team has lost to Manchester United in both of their FA Cup Final appearances, first in a replay in 1990 and second in extra time in 2016?

2. **Netball.** The Storm play their Super League home games in which English county?

*Do you want a home question on Tennis for one point or an away question on Rugby League for two?*

1. **Tennis.** Who was the only Asian tennis player to win a Grand Slam women's singles title between 2015 and 2019?

2. **Rugby League.** In 2013, which four English brothers all played in the same game for the South Sydney Rabbitohs?

*Do you want a home question on Golf for one point or an away question on Gymnastics for two?*

1. **Golf.** Which European golfer became World Number One and won his first and only Major in 1991?

2. **Gymnastics.** On which piece of apparatus did Nadia Comaneci famously score the first ever perfect 10 at the Olympics in 1976?

# Top Ten

**Name the ten teams that have reached the Super Bowl on the most occasions since 1990.**

There's a point for each one you correctly identify, but guess one wrong and you lose your points from this round...

1 ........................................................................

2 ........................................................................

3 ........................................................................

4 ........................................................................

5 ........................................................................

6 ........................................................................

7 ........................................................................

8 ........................................................................

9 ........................................................................

10 ........................................................................

# Buzzer Round

**All the questions in this round are about people called Alex...**

1. Which Alex won gold for Great Britain in Women's Hockey at the Rio 2016 Olympics?

2. At the 2019 Women's World Cup, Alex Morgan scored five goals in one match for which country?

3. Great Britain's Alex Gregory is a double Olympic champion in which rowing event?

4. Snooker World Champion Alex Higgins was known by what nickname?

5. Alex Goode won European Rugby Player of the Year whilst playing for which team?

6. Alex Rodriguez spent the last 12 seasons of his career with which baseball team?

7. Which British Heavyweight boxer defeated Alexander Povetkin in 2018?

8. Formula One driver Alexander Albon moved from Toro Rosso to which other team in 2019?

9. In which sport has Alex Zanardi won four gold medals at the Paralympics?

10. In 2018, Alex Noren became the tenth golfer from which country to represent Europe at the Ryder Cup?

# Sprint Finish

**Describe these ten sporting words
and phrases to your team...**

1. Referee

2. Swimming goggles

3. Boris Becker

4. Snowboarding

5. Closing ceremony

6. Boxing shorts

7. Chris Gayle

8. Back nine

9. London Broncos

10. Black belt

# Game 2 Answers

**One-Minute Round**

1. Leicester Tigers; 2. 15 Reds and 15 Blacks in a Maximum Break; 3. Volleyball;
4. Lionel Messi; 5. 2002; 6. 24; 7. Croatia; 8. Justin ROSE, DAISY Melhuish,
Dennis LILLEE

**Mystery Guest**

Kelly Holmes, Shane Warne

**Home or Away**

1. Rugby Union. Josh Adams
2. Motor Sport. Moto GP

1. Football. Crystal Palace
2. Netball. Surrey

1. Tennis. Naomi Osaka
2. Rugby League. Burgess Brothers

1. Golf. Ian Woosnam
2. Gymnastics. Uneven Bars

**Top Ten**

New England Patriots
Denver Broncos
New York Giants
Pittsburgh Steelers
Buffalo Bills
Dallas Cowboys
Green Bay Packers
San Francisco 49ers
Seattle Seahawks
LA Rams

**Buzzer Round**

1. Alex Danson; 2. USA; 3. Coxless Four; 4. Hurricane; 5. Saracens; 6. New York
Yankees; 7. Anthony Joshua; 8. Red Bull; 9. Paracycling (accept cycling);
10. Sweden

# Game 3

# One-Minute Round

1. Which baseball team play their home games at Wrigley Field?

2. Can you solve this sporting equation? '13PLT for SAF'

3. In which sport would you find the baulk line at the Crucible?

4. 'COY CAMP' is an anagram of which person?

5. In which year did South Africa win their first Rugby Union World Cup?

6. How many players are there in a netball team?

7. Agustin Pichot and Gabriela Sabatini have both competed internationally for which country?

8. These three sports stars all share parts of their names with types of herbs…

   **?** D'Oliveira (Cricket)
   **?** Kotsenburg (Snowboarding)
   Shaquille **?** (Athletics)

# Mystery Guest

**In this round you are given three clues
to a sports star's identity.**

*Who is this Mystery Guest?*

1.   I made my debut at the Crucible in 1993.

2.   I compiled the fastest competitive maximum break in 1997, coming up against Mick Price.

3.   In 2013, I won my fifth World Championship title.

*Who is this Mystery Guest?*

1.   In 2016, I became the third man to hold all four Grand Slam singles titles at once.

2.   I am known for doing impressions of my fellow players on tour.

3.   I'm the first Serbian man to be ranked world number one.

# Home or Away

In this round there is a choice of a home question
for one point or an away question for two.

*Do you want a home question on Football for one point or an
away question on Formula One for two?*

1. **Football.** Who reached the 2018 World Cup Final before going on
   to become the first person from his country to win the Ballon d'Or
   later in the same year?

2. **Formula One.** Which Formula One circuit has the shortest lap in
   terms of distance?

*Do you want a home question on Golf for one point or an away
question on Horse Racing for two?*

1. **Golf.** Who became the first Canadian golfer to win a men's major,
   doing so at the 2003 Masters?

2. **Horse Racing.** The three races that make up the American Triple
   Crown are the Kentucky Derby, the Preakness Stakes and which
   other race?

*Do you want a home question on Athletics for one point or an away question on Darts for two?*

1.  **Athletics.** Which Swede won three consecutive Heptathlon World Championship gold medals between 2003 and 2007, as well as the Olympic title in Athens?

2.  **Darts.** In 2015, who became the first Scotsman to win the PDC Darts World Championships, beating Phil Taylor in the final?

*Do you want a home question on Rugby Union for one point or an away question on the Olympics for two?*

1.  **Rugby Union.** Which hooker became the first player to start in two World Cup Finals, doing so in 1987 and 1995?

2.  **The Olympics.** Since Table Tennis was introduced to the Olympics, which country has won 28 of the 32 gold medals on offer?

# Top Ten

**Name the ten batsmen that have scored
over 11,000 runs in Test cricket.**

There's a point for each one you correctly identify, but guess one
wrong and you lose your points from this round...

1 .................................................................

2 .................................................................

3 .................................................................

4 .................................................................

5 .................................................................

6 .................................................................

7 .................................................................

8 .................................................................

9 .................................................................

10 ................................................................

# Buzzer Round

**The answers to all the questions in this round begin
with the letter G. In the case of a person it's the
surname that will begin with that letter...**

1. What is the franchise name of the NBA team based in Memphis?

2. In 2017, who became the third Spanish golfer to win the US Masters?

3. Which team won cricket's County Championship in 1997?

4. Which famous horse race at Cheltenham did Best Mate win three years in a row?

5. Which British city hosted the 2014 Commonwealth Games?

6. Who won the last of her seven Wimbledon Ladies' Singles titles in 1996?

7. Mikaela Shiffrin won gold at the 2018 Winter Olympics in which skiing event?

8. In which sport have Nadia Comaneci and Olga Korbut both won Olympic gold medals?

9. Which scrum-half won his 139th and final cap for Australia in 2007?

10. Which English football team play their home games at Priestfield Stadium?

# Sprint Finish

**Describe these ten sporting words
and phrases to your team...**

1.  Spin bowler

2.  Offside flag

3.  Donovan Bailey

4.  High tackle

5.  Blackburn Rovers

6.  Nine-dart finish

7.  Equestrian

8.  Gail Emms

9.  Shot put

10. Tug of war

# Game 3 Answers

**One-Minute Round**

1. Chicago Cubs; 2. 13 Premier League Titles for Sir Alex Ferguson;
3. Snooker; 4. AP McCoy; 5. 1995; 6. Seven; 7. Argentina; 8. BASIL D'Oliveira,
SAGE Kotsenburg, Shaquille DILL

**Mystery Guest**

Ronnie O'Sullivan, Novak Djokovic

**Home or Away**

1. Football. Luka Modrić
2. Formula One. Monaco Grand Prix

1. Golf. Mike Weir
2. Horse Racing. Belmont Stakes

1. Athletics. Carolina Klüft
2. Darts. Gary Anderson

1. Rugby Union. Sean Fitzpatrick
2. The Olympics. China

**Top Ten**

Sachin Tendulkar
Ricky Ponting
Jacques Kallis
Rahul Dravid
Alastair Cook
Kumar Sangakkara
Brian Lara
Shivnarine Chanderpaul
Mahela Jayawardene
Allan Border

**Buzzer Round**

1. Grizzlies; 2. Sergio García; 3. Glamorgan; 4. Gold Cup; 5. Glasgow;
6. Steffi Graf; 7. Giant Slalom; 8. Gymnastics; 9. George Gregan; 10. Gillingham

# Game 4

# One-Minute Round

1. Which cricket county play their home games at Edgbaston?

2. Can you solve this sporting equation? '4WT for AP in FO'

3. In which sport would you score points with a *waza-ari*?

4. 'HUN GIRL' is an anagram of which sport?

5. In which year did Rafael Nadal beat Roger Federer to win his first Wimbledon title?

6. David Beckham wore which number at Real Madrid and LA Galaxy?

7. Brianne Theisen-Eaton and Steve Nash have both competed internationally for which country?

8. These three sports stars all share parts of their names with types of hat...

   Larry **?** (American Football)
   Bill **?** (Ice Hockey)
   Wenyan **?** (Swimming)

# Mystery Guest

**In this round you are given three clues
to a sports star's identity.**


## *Who is this Mystery Guest?*

1. I won my only Commonwealth gold at the 2006 games.

2. I finished fifth at the 2016 Foxhunter Chase at Cheltenham.

3. I have three Olympic medals: a gold and silver in the sprint, and a gold in the Keirin.


## *Who is this Mystery Guest?*

1. I turned professional in 1989 at the age of 19.

2. In 1994, I became the first player from my country since Gary Player to win a major.

3. My nickname is 'the Big Easy'.

# Home or Away

**In this round there is a choice of a home question
for one point or an away question for two.**

*Do you want a home question on Football for one point or an
away question on the Olympics for two?*

1. **Football.** Which African country shocked World Champions
   France by beating them in the first game of the 2002 World Cup?

2. **The Olympics.** Joe Clarke and Liam Heath won individual
   Olympic gold medals for Great Britain in 2016 in which sport?

*Do you want a home question on Cricket for one point or an away
question on Cycling for two?*

1. **Cricket.** Whose record of most Test matches as captain of England
   did Alastair Cook overtake in 2016?

2. **Cycling.** As of the start of 2020, which British cyclist was second on
   the all-time list of Tour de France stage wins with 30?

*Do you want a home question on Tennis for one point or an away question on American Football for two?*

1.  **Tennis.** Which woman was undefeated in singles matches on clay for 125 matches between 1973 and 1979?

2.  **American Football.** The Vince Lombardi trophy is named after the coach of which team that won the first two Super Bowls?

*Do you want a home question on Athletics for one point or an away question on Snooker for two?*

1.  **Athletics.** Over which distance did Ethiopian Haile Gebrselassie win two Olympic and four World Championship gold medals?

2.  **Snooker.** Who is the only player to have won and lost in World Snooker Championship finals against Stephen Hendry?

# Top Ten

**As of the start of 2020, name the ten teams that have reached the FA Cup Final on the most occasions.**

There's a point for each one you correctly identify, but guess one wrong and you lose your points from this round...

1  ...........................................................................

2  ...........................................................................

3  ...........................................................................

4  ...........................................................................

5  ...........................................................................

6  ...........................................................................

7  ...........................................................................

8  ...........................................................................

9  ...........................................................................

10 ...........................................................................

# Buzzer Round

**All the questions in this round are about the colour red or have red in the answer**

1. In Snooker, how many red balls are on the table at the start of a frame?

2. Rugby Union side Queensland Reds play their home games in which Australian city?

3. The red jersey signifies the leader of the general classification in which of cycling's Grand Tours?

4. Which British Formula One driver famously raced with a red number five on his car in the 1980s and 1990s?

5. Against which country was David Beckham shown a red card at the 1998 World Cup?

6. Which Boston based team won the first ever World Series in 1903?

7. In what year did Red Rum win the last of his three Grand Nationals at Aintree?

8. Which Grand Slam tennis tournament is competed on red clay?

9. Steve Redgrave teamed up with which rower to win three of his Olympic gold medals?

10. In which sport have the Cincinnati Reds won five World Series titles?

# Sprint Finish

**Describe these ten sporting words
and phrases to your team...**

1. Michael Jordan

2. Drinks break

3. St Andrews

4. Corner flag

5. San Siro

6. Yellow jersey

7. Netball

8. Straight sets

9. Royal Ascot

10. Commonwealth Games

# **Game 4** Answers

**One-Minute Round**
1. Warwickshire; 2. 4 World Titles for Alain Prost in Formula One; 3. Judo;
4. Hurling; 5. 2008; 6. 23; 7. Canada; 8. Larry FEDORA, Bill BOWLER,
Wenyan SUN

**Mystery Guest**
Victoria Pendleton, Ernie Els

**Home and Away**
1. Football. Senegal
2. The Olympics. Canoeing

1. Cricket. Michael Atherton
2. Cycling. Mark Cavendish

1. Tennis. Chris Evert
2. American Football. Green Bay Packers

1. Athletics. 10,000m
2. Snooker. Peter Ebdon

**Top Ten**
Arsenal
Manchester United
Liverpool
Chelsea
Newcastle United
Everton
Aston Villa
Manchester City
West Bromwich Albion
Tottenham Hotspur

**Buzzer Round**
1. 15; 2. Brisbane; 3. Vuelta a España; 4. Nigel Mansell; 5. Argentina;
6. Boston Red Sox; 7. 1977; 8. French Open; 9. Matthew Pinsent; 10. Baseball

# Game 5

# One-Minute Round

1. Which football team play their home games at the Allianz Arena?

2. Can you solve this sporting equation? '2P and 1H in a FR in RU'

3. In which sport would you use the terms moonball and double bagel?

4. 'TUNA BOILS' is an anagram of which athlete?

5. In which year did the Premier League begin?

6. How many players are in a rugby league team?

7. Sergei Bubka and Andriy Shevchenko have both competed internationally for which country?

8. These three sports stars all share parts of their names with birds you'd find on the water...

   Jenny ? (Hockey)
   Rob ? (Sailing)
   Graeme ? (Cricket)

# Mystery Guest

**In this round you are given three clues
to a sports star's identity.**

### Who is this Mystery Guest?

1.  I started my football career with Sporting Lisbon.

2.  I have played over 150 times for my country, winning the European
    Championship in 2016.

3.  I won the Serie A title in 2019, to add to my three Premier League
    and two La Liga titles.

### Who is this Mystery Guest?

1.  In the 2002, I broke the record for the most winners ridden in
    a season.

2.  In my 15th attempt in the Grand National, I finally won the race
    on Don't Push It in 2010.

3.  I was named the National Hunt Champion Jockey on a record
    20 occasions.

# Home or Away

In this round there is a choice of a home question
for one point or an away question for two.

*Do you want a home question on Cricket for one point or an away
question on Snooker for two?*

1. **Cricket.** Which wicketkeeper, who played in his final Test in 1981,
   holds the record for most dismissals in Test matches for England?

2. **Snooker.** Which of his compatriots did Mark Williams defeat in the
   2000 World Championship Final?

*Do you want a home question on Football for one point or an
away question on Rugby League for two?*

1. **Football.** Which team, who play their home games at the Ali Sami
   Yen, have won the top flight in Turkey a record number of times?

2. **Rugby League.** Who is the only Rugby League player to score over
   3,000 points in Super League?

*Do you want a home question on Tennis for one point or an away question on the Winter Olympics for two?*

1.  **Tennis.** Between 2014 and 2016, which tennis player won the first three Grand Slam men's singles finals he appeared in?

2.  **The Winter Olympics.** In which sport have Alex Coomber, Laura Deas and Dominic Parsons all won Winter Olympic bronze for Great Britain?

*Do you want a home question on Golf for one point or an away question on Basketball for two?*

1.  **Golf.** Which English female golfer won three majors in the 1990s, and has four in total?

2.  **Basketball.** Which team have reached the NBA Finals 21 times, winning on all but four occasions?

# Top Ten

**As of the end of the 2019 season, name the
ten Formula One Grand Prix that have
been held on more than 40 occasions.**

There's a point for each one you correctly identify, but guess one
wrong and you lose your points from this round…

1 ...............................................................

2 ...............................................................

3 ...............................................................

4 ...............................................................

5 ...............................................................

6 ...............................................................

7 ...............................................................

8 ...............................................................

9 ...............................................................

10 ...............................................................

# Buzzer Round

**All the questions in this round
are about the Commonwealth Games...**

1.  Which Asian city hosted the Commonwealth Games in 2010?

2.  In which sport are Nick Matthew and Nicol David both Commonwealth Champions?

3.  Which Northern Irishman won Bantamweight gold at the 1978 Games before becoming World Featherweight Champion in 1985?

4.  Which swimmer won 13 Commonwealth medals in her career and carried the England flag at the 2002 Closing Ceremony?

5.  Which country has won the most medals in the history of the Games?

6.  Helen Housby scored the winning goal as England won a Commonwealth gold for the first time in which sport?

7.  Which 110m hurdler won his first Commonwealth medal in 1986 and his last in 2002?

8.  Which woman won four gymnastics gold medals at the 2014 Games for England?

9.  The Rugby Sevens gold medals have been won on all but one occasion by which country?

10. Scotsman Alex Marshall has won five Commonwealth gold medals in which sport?

# Sprint Finish

**Describe these ten sporting words
and phrases to your team...**

1. Corner pocket

2. Ian Woosnam

3. Team talk

4. Jab

5. Steve Backley

6. Relegation battle

7. Tennis elbow

8. New England Patriots

9. Badminton

10. Saddle

# Game 5 Answers

**One-Minute Round**

1. Bayern Munich; 2. 2 Props and 1 Hooker in a Front Row in Rugby Union;
3. Tennis; 4. Usain Bolt; 5. 1992; 6. 13; 7. Ukraine; 8. Jenny DUCK, Rob CRANE,
Graeme SWANN

**Mystery Guest**

Cristiano Ronaldo, AP McCoy

**Home or Away**

1. Cricket. Alan Knott
2. Snooker. Matthew Stevens

1. Football. Galatasaray
2. Rugby League. Kevin Sinfield

1. Tennis. Stan Wawrinka
2. The Winter Olympics. Skeleton

1. Golf. Laura Davies
2. Basketball. Boston Celtics

**Top Ten**

British Grand Prix
Italian Grand Prix
Monaco Grand Prix
Belgian Grand Prix
German Grand Prix
French Grand Prix
Canadian Grand Prix
Spanish Grand Prix
Brazilian Grand Prix
USA Grand Prix

**Buzzer Round**

1. Delhi; 2. Squash; 3. Barry McGuigan; 4. Karen Pickering; 5. Australia;
6. Netball; 7. Colin Jackson; 8. Claudia Fragapane; 9. New Zealand;
10. Lawn Bowls

# Game 6

# One-Minute Round

1.  Which rugby union team play their home games at Kingsholm?

2.  Can you solve this sporting equation? '40SH in the GN'

3.  In which sport would you compete for the Stanley Cup?

4.  'EARFUL MOON' is an anagram of which sport?

5.  In which year did Tiger Woods win his first major?

6.  How many NBA titles did Michael Jordan win?

7.  Mark Philippoussis and Cathy Freeman have both competed internationally for which country?

8.  These three sports stars all share parts of their names with things you'd find in an office…

    Arthur **?** (Baseball)
    Russell **?** (Football)
    Young **?** (Boxing)

# Mystery Guest

**In this round you are given three clues
to a sports star's identity.**

*Who is this Mystery Guest?*

1.  In 1994, I became the youngest ever All Black.

2.  I won the BBC Overseas Sports Personality of the Year award in 1995 for my World Cup performances.

3.  I share the record for the most World Cup tries, with 15 over two tournaments.

*Who is this Mystery Guest?*

1.  In 2011, I won two golds at the Commonwealth Youth Games for England.

2.  I won three European sprint golds in 2018, followed by World gold the year after.

3.  I set the British female record over 100 and 200m in 2019.

# Home or Away

In this round there is a choice of a home question
for one point or an away question for two.

*Do you want a home question on Tennis for one point or an away
question on Netball for two?*

1. **Tennis.** Which Croatian won the 2014 US Open and four years
   later won the Davis Cup with his country for the first time?

2. **Netball.** Which is the only country to have won a medal at the
   Netball World Cup but has never reached the final, winning bronze
   three times?

*Do you want a home question on Football for one point or an
away question on Cycling for two?*

1. **Football.** Which Englishman scored the first ever goal in the
   Premier League when he netted for Sheffield United in 1992?

2. **Cycling.** In 2018, who became the fourth consecutive British
   winner of the Tour De France, by winning the race for the first time
   in his career?

*Do you want a home question on Cricket for one point or an away question on Boxing for two?*

1. **Cricket.** Who in 2017, captained the England Women's cricket team to World Cup glory, for the first time since 1993?

2. **Boxing.** World Champion boxers Thomas Hearns and Ricky Hatton share which nickname?

*Do you want a home question on Rugby Union for one point or an away question on Motor Sport for two?*

1. **Rugby Union.** Who has captained England on the most occasions in test rugby, the first time in 1988 and the last in 1996?

2. **Motor Sport.** In 2019, which Northern Irishman became the first rider to win the Superbike World Championship five times?

# Top Ten

**Name the ten European golfers to win a
men's major between 2010 and 2019.**

There's a point for each one you correctly identify, but guess one
wrong and you lose your points from this round...

1 ........................................................

2 ........................................................

3 ........................................................

4 ........................................................

5 ........................................................

6 ........................................................

7 ........................................................

8 ........................................................

9 ........................................................

10 ........................................................

# Buzzer Round

**All the questions in this round are about
Asia and sports stars from that continent...**

1.  Which Asian city hosted the 2019 World Athletics Championships?

2.  The Japanese Rugby Union team are nicknamed what, in relation to their national flower?

3.  At which tournament in 2011 did Chinese tennis player Li Na win her first ever Grand Slam?

4.  Which Kazakh boxer drew with Canelo Álvarez in 2017, before losing the rematch a year later?

5.  Formula One's first ever night race took place in which country?

6.  Chinese basketball player Yao Ming played for which Texan NBA side?

7.  Who is the only bowler to take 400 Test wickets for Pakistan?

8.  Which country has won a record eight Olympic gold medals in men's field hockey?

9.  In what year did South Korea and Japan co-host the FIFA World Cup?

10. Who, in 2005, was the first Asian snooker player to win the UK Championship?

# Sprint Finish

**Describe these ten sporting words
and phrases to your team...**

1. Stamford Bridge

2. Headguard

3. Jessica Ennis-Hill

4. Run out

5. National Anthem

6. Vice-captain

7. Martina Hingis

8. FA Cup

9. Punt

10. Starting grid

# **Game 6** Answers

---

### One-Minute Round

1. Gloucester; 2. 40 Starting Horses in the Grand National; 3. Ice hockey;
4. Formula One; 5. 1997; 6. Six; 7. Australia; 8. Arthur STAPLES, Russell PENN,
Young MUG

### Mystery Guest

Jonah Lomu, Dina Asher-Smith

### Home or Away

1.  Tennis. Marin Čilić
2.  Netball. Jamaica

1.  Football. Brian Deane
2.  Cycling. Geraint Thomas

1.  Cricket. Heather Knight
2.  Boxing. Hitman

1.  Rugby Union. Will Carling
2.  Motor Sport. Jonathan Rea

### Top Ten

Graeme McDowell
Martin Kaymer
Rory McIlroy
Darren Clarke
Justin Rose
Danny Willett
Henrik Stenson
Sergio Garcia
Francesco Molinari
Shane Lowry

### Buzzer Round

1. Doha; 2. Cherry Blossoms; 3. French Open; 4. Gennady Golovkin; 5. Singapore;
6. Houston Rockets; 7. Wasim Akram; 8. India; 9. 2002; 10. Ding Junhui

# Game 7

# One-Minute Round

1. Which football team play their home games at the Westfalenstadion?

2. Can you solve this sporting equation? '8 = WST for RF'

3. In which sport would you hear 'the hammer' and 'forehand draw'?

4. 'RIO KOALA CAST' is an anagram of which cricketer?

5. In which year did Roger Bannister run the first four-minute mile?

6. What number does a tighthead prop wear in Rugby Union?

7. Janine Flock and Franz Klammer have both competed internationally for which country?

8. These three sports stars all share parts of their names with Mr Men…

   **?** Williams (American Football)
   Danny **?** (Rugby League)
   Jamal **?** (Baseball)

# Mystery Guest

**In this round you are given three clues
to a sports star's identity.**

### Who is this Mystery Guest?

1.  I became World Champion at the age of 39.

2.  I am the only driver to have been the F1 World Champion and Indy Car Champion simultaneously.

3.  I won the BBC Sports Personality of the Year in 1986 and 1992.

### Who is this Mystery Guest?

1.  I started my NFL career in the year 2000.

2.  I won the Super Bowl for a sixth time in 2019.

3.  In 2020, I joined a Florida-based NFL team after 20 years with my previous organisation.

# Home or Away

**In this round there is a choice of a home question
for one point or an away question for two.**

*Do you want a home question on Cricket for one point or an away
question on Swimming for two?*

1.  **Cricket.** In 2003, who became the captain of his country at just
    22, before scoring double hundreds in consecutive Tests against
    England?

2.  **Swimming.** In 2011, which British swimmer retained the Open
    Water Swimming World Title that she won two years earlier?

*Do you want a home question on Golf for one point or an away
question on Baseball for two?*

1.  **Golf.** On which Spanish golf course did Seve Ballesteros captain
    Europe to victory in the 1997 Ryder Cup?

2.  **Baseball.** Which team hold the record for the most World Series
    won in Major League Baseball history?

*Do you want a home question on Football for one point or an away question on Snooker for two?*

1. **Football.** Which African country beat Argentina at the 1990 World Cup before being knocked out by England in the quarter-finals?

2. **Snooker.** In 1998, who became only the second Scotsman to win the World Snooker Championship at the Crucible?


*Do you want a home question on Tennis for one point or an away question on Horse Racing for two?*

1. **Tennis.** In 2019, which Greek tennis player won the ATP Tour Finals in London, as well as reaching his first Grand Slam semi-final at the Australian Open?

2. **Horse Racing.** Between 2010 and 2012, jockey Tom Queally rode which horse to victory in all 14 of its races, and in doing so helped it become the highest-rated horse in the world?

# Top Ten

**Not including Tokyo, name the ten most recent hosts of the Summer Olympics.**

There's a point for each one you correctly identify, but guess one wrong and you lose your points from this round…

1 .......................................................................

2 .......................................................................

3 .......................................................................

4 .......................................................................

5 .......................................................................

6 .......................................................................

7 .......................................................................

8 .......................................................................

9 .......................................................................

10 ......................................................................

# Buzzer Round

**All the questions in this round are about people whose surnames are Johnson...**

1. With which club did Glen Johnson win the FA Cup in 2008?

2. Michael Johnson won the last of his last Olympic gold medals at which games?

3. In 2011, who took over from Martin Johnson as head coach of the England Rugby Union team?

4. With which basketball team did Magic Johnson win five NBA Championships in the 1980s?

5. Which title did Richard Johnson finally win in 2016, having finished runner up to AP McCoy on 16 occasions?

6. Which Johnson has taken over 300 Test wickets for Australia?

7. Golfer Dustin Johnson won the first major of his career in 2016 by winning which tournament?

8. Steve Davis lost the 1986 World Snooker Championship Final to which player?

9. Gymnast Shawn Johnson won Olympic gold on the balance beam in 2008 for which country?

10. In 2019, Katarina Johnson-Thompson won World Championship gold in which athletics event?

# Sprint Finish

**Describe these ten sporting words
and phrases to your team...**

1. Scrum

2. Pole position

3. Jade Jones

4. Swansea City

5. Maximum break

6. Interception

7. Wrestling

8. Coin toss

9. Gary Lineker

10. Starting blocks

# **Game 7** Answers

### **One-Minute Round**

1. Borussia Dortmund; 2. 8 = Wimbledon Singles Titles for Roger Federer;
3. Bowls; 4. Alastair Cook; 5. 1954; 6. Three; 7. Austria; 8. GREEDY Williams,
Danny TICKLE, Jamal STRONG

### **Mystery Guest**

Nigel Mansell, Tom Brady

### **Home or Away**

1. Cricket. Graeme Smith
2. Swimming. Keri-Anne Payne

1. Golf. Valderrama
2. Baseball. New York Yankees

1. Football. Cameroon
2. Snooker. John Higgins

1. Tennis. Stefanos Tsitsipas
2. Horse Racing. Frankel

### **Top Ten**

Rio de Janeiro
London
Beijing
Athens
Sydney
Atlanta
Barcelona
Seoul
Los Angeles
Moscow

### **Buzzer Round**

1. Portsmouth; 2. Sydney 2000; 3. Stuart Lancaster; 4. LA Lakers; 5. Champion
Jockey; 6. Mitchell Johnson; 7. US Open; 8. Joe Johnson; 9. USA; 10. Heptathlon

# Game 8

# One-Minute Round

1. Which Rugby Union team play their home games at the Twickenham Stoop?

2. Can you solve this sporting equation? '91FOW for MS'

3. In which sport could you have a 'penalty flick' and receive a green card?

4. 'WET IF LIGHTING' is an anagram of which sport?

5. In which year did boxing's 'Rumble in the Jungle' happen?

6. How many FIFA World Cups have Italy won?

7. Shelly-Ann Fraser-Pryce and Robbie Earle have both competed internationally for which country?

8. These three sports stars all share parts of their names with famous English universities...

   Reece **?** (Football)
   Ray **?** (Baseball)
   Asuka **?** (Athletics)

# Mystery Guest

**In this round you are given three clues
to a sports star's identity.**

## Who is this Mystery Guest?

1. I was born in Leeds in 1982.

2. I went undefeated in my six professional fights, before retiring in 2019.

3. In 2016, I was the first female to successfully defend an Olympic title at flyweight.

## Who is this Mystery Guest?

1. I made my England Test debut in Nagpur in 2012, aged 21.

2. In England's one-day and T20 matches, I wear the number 66.

3. I became captain of England's Test cricket team when Alastair Cook stepped down in February 2017.

# Home or Away

**In this round there is a choice of a home question
for one point or an away question for two.**

*Do you want a home question on Football for one point or an
away question on Horse Racing for two?*

1.  **Football.** Who became the youngest player since Gareth Barry to
    make 500 appearances in the Premier League?

2.  **Horse Racing.** Flemington Racecourse plays host to which annual
    Australian horse race?

*Do you want a home question on Golf for one point or an away
question on the Olympics for two?*

1.  **Golf.** Six different women from which country have captained
    Europe in golf's Solheim Cup?

2.  **The Olympics.** Who won the last of his four Olympic gold medals
    in 2004, having won his first partnering Steve Redgrave?

*Do you want a home question on Rugby Union for one point or an away question on Snooker for two?*

1. **Rugby Union.** Which English winger scored a try in the 2017 Premiership Final victory for his club, and then won two caps for the Lions later that summer?

2. **Snooker.** Which Scotsman reached the World Championship final three times between 2000 and 2010, winning once and losing the other two?

*Do you want a home question on Athletics for one point or an away question on Darts for two?*

1. **Athletics.** Since 2000, London and which other city have hosted both the Olympics and the World Athletics Championships?

2. **Darts.** In 2019, who beat Ted Evetts to become the first woman to win a match at the PDC World Darts Championships?

# Top Ten

**Name the first ten women to top the World Rankings in tennis. The rankings began in 1975.**

There's a point for each one you correctly identify, but guess one wrong and you lose your points from this round...

1 ................................................................

2 ................................................................

3 ................................................................

4 ................................................................

5 ................................................................

6 ................................................................

7 ................................................................

8 ................................................................

9 ................................................................

10 ................................................................

# Buzzer Round

**All the questions in this round are about sport in the 1990s...**

1. Who beat England in the 1991 Rugby Union World Cup Final?

2. Who won the Tour de France five times in the 1990s?

3. Which country both won and lost in a men's FIFA World Cup Final in the decade?

4. Which British rider won his fourth and final Superbike World Championship in 1999?

5. Which team won the Super Bowl three times in the 1990s?

6. Where did Tiger Woods win his first major?

7. In 1994, who became boxing's oldest heavyweight champion when he beat Michael Moorer at the age of 45?

8. Which extreme sport made its Winter Olympic debut at the 1998 games in Nagano?

9. In 1996, which Rugby League team won the first ever Super League season?

10. The USA Basketball team that played in the 1992 and 1996 Summer Olympics had what nickname?

# Sprint Finish

**Describe these ten sporting words
and phrases to your team...**

1.  Bullseye

2.  Table tennis

3.  Triple crown

4.  Ian Botham

5.  Breaststroke

6.  Crossbar

7.  Dead heat

8.  Sheffield United

9.  Pole vault

10. Wetsuit

# **Game 8** Answers

---

**One-Minute Round**

1. Harlequins; 2. 91 Formula One Wins for Michael Schumacher; 3. Hockey;
4. Weightlifting; 5. 1974; 6. Four; 7. Jamaica; 8. Reece OXFORD,
Ray DURHAM, Asuka CAMBRIDGE

**Mystery Guest**

Nicola Adams, Joe Root

**Home or Away**

1. Football. James Milner
2. Horse Racing. Melbourne Cup

1. Golf. Sweden
2. The Olympics. Matthew Pinsent

1. Rugby Union. Jack Nowell
2. Snooker. Graeme Dott

1. Athletics. Beijing
2. Darts. Fallon Sherrock

**Top Ten**

Chris Evert
Evonne Goolagong Cawley
Martina Navratilova
Tracy Austin
Steffi Graf
Monica Seles
Arantxa Sánchez Vicario
Martina Hingis
Lindsay Davenport
Jennifer Capriati

**Buzzer Round**

1. Australia; 2. Miguel Induráin; 3. Brazil; 4. Carl Fogarty; 5. Dallas Cowboys;
6. US Masters at Augusta; 7. George Foreman; 8. Snowboarding; 9. St Helens;
10. Dream Team

# Game 9

# One-Minute Round

1. Which county cricket team play their home games at Old Trafford?

2. Can you solve this sporting equation? '7PLT for PC'

3. In which aquatic sport would you perform a 'tuck' and a 'pike'?

4. 'MYSTIC NAGS' is an anagram of which sport?

5. In which year did Australian Pat Cash win Wimbledon?

6. How many points are awarded for a try in Rugby League?

7. Pau Gasol and Mireia Belmonte have both competed internationally for which country?

8. These three sports stars all share parts of their names with things you find in the sky…

   Tavoris **?** (Boxing)
   Jackson **?** (Cricket)
   Tom **?** (Golf)

# Mystery Guest

**In this round you are given three clues
to a sports star's identity.**

### Who is this Mystery Guest?

1.  I am known as one of Europe's most enigmatic golfers.

2.  I formed a famous partnership with José María Olazábal in the Ryder Cup.

3.  I won five majors in my career, my last coming at The Open in 1988.

### Who is this Mystery Guest?

1.  I was the first teenager since Lester Piggott to win 100 races in a season.

2.  I'm well known for my flying dismounts.

3.  I was a captain on *A Question of Sport* in the 2000s.

# Home or Away

**In this round there is a choice of a home question
for one point or an away question for two.**

*Do you want a home question on Cricket for one point or an away
question on Formula One for two?*

1.  **Cricket.** In 2010, with his last wicket in Test cricket, Sri Lankan
    spinner Muttiah Muralitharan became the first person to pass what
    milestone in Tests?

2.  **Formula One.** In 2008, which driver finished one point behind
    eventual World Champion Lewis Hamilton, despite winning the last
    race of the season at his home Grand Prix?

*Do you want a home question on Football for one point or an
away question on the Olympics for two?*

1.  **Football.** Who scored 60 goals for QPR in the first three
    Premier League seasons, helping them to a top ten finish in each
    of those years?

2.  **The Olympics.** Who partnered Heather Stanning as she won
    rowing gold in the coxless pairs in 2012 and then retained the title
    four years later?

*Do you want a home question on Tennis for one point or an away question on Basketball for two?*

1.  **Tennis.** Who reached the US Open men's singles final for eight consecutive years during the 1980s, winning the title on three occasions?

2.  **Basketball.** Which Western Conference team played in five consecutive NBA championships between 2015 and 2019?

*Do you want a home question on Athletics for one point or an away question on the Commonwealth Games for two?*

1.  **Athletics.** Which British wheelchair racer won three gold medals in the T34 class at the Rio Paralympics?

2.  **Commonwealth Games.** In 1998, in which city did Ten Pin Bowling feature at the Commonwealth Games for the only time?

# Top Ten

**As of the start of the 2020 season, name the ten Rugby Union teams that have won the most games in the Premiership?**

There's a point for each one you correctly identify, but guess one wrong and you lose your points from this round…

1 .......................................................................

2 .......................................................................

3 .......................................................................

4 .......................................................................

5 .......................................................................

6 .......................................................................

7 .......................................................................

8 .......................................................................

9 .......................................................................

10 .......................................................................

# Buzzer Round

**The answers to all the questions in this round begin with the letter A. In the case of a person it's the surname that will begin with that letter...**

1. Which cricketer became the first Englishman to take 500 Test wickets?

2. In which Olympic sport would you 'nock' and 'draw' from a distance of 70m?

3. In which New Zealand city was the first Rugby Union World Cup Final held?

4. Who captained the USA to Ryder Cup victory in 2008?

5. Which football team won the European Cup three times in a row between 1971 and 1973?

6. Which tennis player won eight Grand Slam singles titles in his career, including Wimbledon in 1992?

7. Yeats won the Gold Cup four years in a row between 2006 and 2009 on which racecourse?

8. Which 1978 Formula One World Champion is the last American driver to win the title?

9.  What is the franchise name of the Major League Baseball team based in Houston that won the World Series in 2017?

10. Marcel Hirscher is a double Olympic skiing champion from which country?

# Sprint Finish

**Describe these ten sporting words
and phrases to your team...**

1. Flushing Meadows

2. Deadline Day

3. 100m Hurdles

4. Eoin Morgan

5. Luge

6. Personal best

7. Penalty corner

8. Safety car

9. New York Knicks

10. Uppercut

# **Game 9** Answers

### One-Minute Round

1. Lancashire; 2. 7 Premier League Teams for Peter Crouch; 3. Diving;
4. Gymnastics; 5. 1987; 6. Four; 7. Spain; 8. Tavoris CLOUD, Jackson BIRD,
Tom KITE

### Mystery Guest

Seve Ballesteros, Frankie Dettori

### Home or Away

1. Cricket. 800 Test wickets
2. Formula One. Felipe Massa

1. Football. Les Ferdinand
2. The Olympics. Helen Glover

1. Tennis. Ivan Lendl
2. Basketball. Golden State Warriors

1. Athletics. Hannah Cockroft
2. Commonwealth Games. Kuala Lumpur

### Top Ten

Leicester Tigers
Saracens
London Wasps
Bath
Northampton Saints
Gloucester
Sale Sharks
Harlequins
London Irish
Newcastle Falcons

### Buzzer Round

1. James Anderson; 2. Archery; 3. Auckland; 4. Paul Azinger; 5. Ajax;
6. Andre Agassi; 7. Ascot; 8. Mario Andretti; 9. Astros; 10. Austria

# Game 10

# One-Minute Round

1. Which Rugby League team play their home games at Headingley?

2. Can you solve this sporting equation? '12FT in the SP'

3. In which sport would you see a 'silly point' and a 'fine leg'?

4. 'RIDER LIFTS CHINO' is an anagram of which British athlete?

5. In which year did Chris Froome first win the Tour de France?

6. How many races were there in the 2019 Formula One season?

7. Angelos Charisteas and Stefanos Tsitsipas have both played internationally for which country?

8. These three sports stars all share parts of their names with things you'd find at a restaurant…

   Roger-Phillipe **?** (Swimming)
   Otto **?** (Water Polo)
   Van **?** (American Football)

# Mystery Guest

**In this round you are given three clues
to a sports star's identity.**

### Who is this Mystery Guest?

1.  I made my England Test debut at Lord's in 2003.

2.  I have been 'not out' more times than any other player in
    Test cricket.

3.  I hold the record for the most Test wickets taken by a pace bowler.

### Who is this Mystery Guest?

1.  I won six titles in seven years with my team in the 1990s.

2.  I have been immortalised on my own brand of trainers since 1984.

3.  I starred in the 1996 film *Space Jam* alongside Bugs Bunny.

# Home or Away

**In this round there is a choice of a home question
for one point or an away question for two.**

*Do you want a home question on Golf for one point or an away
question on the Winter Olympics for two?*

1. **Golf.** In 2009, Tom Watson nearly became the oldest major
   champion in history at 59, but which of his compatriots did he lose
   to in the Open Championship playoff?

2. **Winter Olympics.** In which city did Torvill and Dean win Winter
   Olympic gold for their *Boléro* routine?

*Do you want a home question on Football for one point or an
away question on Swimming for two?*

1. **Football.** Which team beat Manchester City 1–0 in the 2013
   FA Cup Final, but were also relegated from the Premier League
   that season?

2. **Swimming.** Who was the only swimmer to win gold for Great
   Britain at the 1980 Olympics, doing so in the 100m breaststroke?

*Do you want a home question on Athletics for one point or an away question on Formula One for two?*

1. **Athletics.** Between 1992 and 1994, which British athlete broke a World Record and won Olympic, World, European and Commonwealth gold, all in the 400m hurdles?

2. **Formula One.** Between 1995 and 2001, which driver finished in the top three of the Formula One World Championship on five occasions, without winning the title?

*Do you want a home question on Rugby Union for one point or an away question on Darts for two?*

1. **Rugby Union.** Who, in 1998, became the first English team to win the Heineken Cup, but have only got past the quarter-final stage once since then?

2. **Darts.** In 2003, which Canadian became the first non-English player to win the PDC Darts World Championship?

# Top Ten

___

**Name the ten countries that have won the UEFA European Championships?**

There's a point for each one you correctly identify, but guess one wrong and you lose your points from this round…

1 ............................................................

2 ............................................................

3 ............................................................

4 ............................................................

5 ............................................................

6 ............................................................

7 ............................................................

8 ............................................................

9 ............................................................

10 ............................................................

# Buzzer Round

**All the questions in this round are about debuts and firsts...**

1. Table tennis made its Summer Olympics debut in Seoul, in which year?

2. In 2003, golfer Ben Curtis, ranked 396th in the world, won which major on his debut appearance?

3. Graham Thorpe made an Ashes century on his England Test debut, at which Midlands cricket ground?

4. In 2018, which Irish winger finished his debut Six Nations campaign as the competition's leading try scorer?

5. Which city hosted the first modern Summer Olympics in 1896?

6. Which Canadian beat Serena Williams in the 2019 US Open Final at her first attempt in the competition?

7. The PDC Darts Championship was held at which London venue for the first time in 2008?

8. Which English defender scored an own goal and was sent off on his debut for Real Madrid in 2005?

9. Liam Treadwell won the 2009 Grand National at Aintree in his first appearance in the race riding which rank outsider?

10. In 2020, which team became the first North American club to play in Rugby League's Super League?

# Sprint Finish

**Describe these ten sporting words
and phrases to your team...**

1. Diamond League

2. Equaliser

3. Back swing

4. Billie Jean King

5. Wooden spoon

6. Epsom Derby

7. Hail Mary

8. High jump

9. Water skiing

10. Michael Vaughan

# **Game 10** Answers

### One-Minute Round
1. Leeds Rhinos; 2. 12 Football Teams in the Scottish Premiership; 3. Cricket;
4. Linford Christie; 5. 2013; 6. 21; 7. Greece; 8. Roger-Phillipe MENU,
Otto SCHEFF, Van WAITERS

### Mystery Guest
James Anderson, Michael Jordan

### Home or Away
1. Golf. Stewart Cink
2. Winter Olympics. Sarajevo

1. Football. Wigan Athletic
2. Swimming. Duncan Goodhew

1. Athletics. Sally Gunnell
2. Formula One. David Coulthard

1. Rugby Union. Bath
2. Darts. John Part

### Top Ten
Soviet Union (accept Russia)
Spain
Italy
Germany
Czechoslovakia
France
Netherlands
Denmark
Greece
Portugal

### Buzzer Round
1. 1988; 2. The Open Championship; 3. Trent Bridge; 4. Jacob Stockdale;
5. Athens; 6. Bianca Andreescu; 7. Alexandra Palace; 8. Jonathan Woodgate;
9. Mon Mome; 10. Toronto Wolfpack

# Game 11

# One-Minute Round

1. Which football team play their home games at Deepdale?

2. Can you solve this sporting equation? '12R in MPB'

3. In which race would you encounter the Canal Turn and the Chair?

4. 'ALE STITCH' is an anagram of which sport?

5. In which year did the longest ever match at Wimbledon take place?

6. How many points are scored in a maximum break in snooker?

7. Jonas Jerebko and Henrik Stenson have both played internationally for which country?

8. These three sports stars all share parts of their names with noises farmyard animals make…

   Moana **?** Caille (BMX)
   Demba **?** (Football)
   **?** Lopez (Weightlifting)

# Mystery Guest

**In this round you are given three clues
to a sports star's identity.**

## Who is this Mystery Guest?

1. I won Olympic gold in 1960 under a name I changed four years later.

2. A biographical film following ten years of my life was made in 2001 starring Will Smith.

3. I competed in the Rumble in the Jungle and the Thriller in Manila.

## Who is this Mystery Guest?

1. I was appointed chair of UK Sport in 2017.

2. I have won silver medals at four Olympic Games.

3. I won gold at the 2012 Olympics in the Double Sculls partnering Anna Watkins.

# Home or Away

In this round there is a choice of a home question
for one point or an away question for two.

*Do you want a home question on Football for one point or an
away question on Rugby League for two?*

1.  **Football.** Whose 128th and final appearance for England came in
    the 1990 FIFA World Cup third place playoff match?

2.  **Rugby League.** Who, in 1993, became the youngest player to play
    in a Challenge Cup final, and then three years later became the
    youngest ever captain of Great Britain?

*Do you want a home question on Golf for one point or an away
question on the Olympics for two?*

1.  **Golf.** Held since 1994, in which golf tournament do the USA play an
    international team, excluding Europe, every two years?

2.  **The Olympics.** After lighting the flame at her home Olympics in
    2000, who went on to win an Olympic gold medal by winning the
    women's 400m?

*Do you want a home question on Rugby Union for one point or an away question on Swimming for two?*

1. **Rugby Union.** Who kicked a penalty in his last game for New Zealand to help them win the 2011 World Cup final, despite not being named in the original squad?

2. **Swimming.** Between 1990 and 2002, which female swimmer won 13 Commonwealth medals in the pool for England?

*Do you want a home question on Tennis for one point or an away question on Boxing for two?*

1. **Tennis.** Who became the first woman from a Scandinavian country to top the WTA World Rankings?

2. **Boxing.** Which member of the Fabulous Four won gold at the 1976 Olympics before becoming World Champion at five different weights?

# Top Ten

**Name the ten teams in cricket's
County Championship that end in '-shire'.**

There's a point for each one you correctly identify, but guess one
wrong and you lose your points from this round…

1 .........................................................................

2 .........................................................................

3 .........................................................................

4 .........................................................................

5 .........................................................................

6 .........................................................................

7 .........................................................................

8 .........................................................................

9 .........................................................................

10 ........................................................................

# Buzzer Round

**All the questions in this round are about
Germany and sports stars from that country...**

1. Which German city hosted the 1972 Olympics?

2. With which team did German Michael Schumacher win his first two
   Formula One World Championships?

3. In which sport is Tony Martin a multiple World Champion?

4. Steffi Graf won her first Wimbledon title in which year?

5. Which golfer won the Masters in 1985 and 1993?

6. Jürgen Klinsmann scored 29 Premier League goals for which club?

7. Heike Drechsler won Olympic gold in 1992 and 2000 in which
   field event?

8. German basketball star Dirk Nowitzki was named the 2011 Final
   MVP with which Texas-based team?

9. In which city did German figure skater Katarina Witt win Winter
   Olympic gold in 1988?

10. In which sport have the German men's team won gold at the 1992,
    2008 and 2012 Olympics?

# Sprint Finish

**Describe these ten sporting words
and phrases to your team...**

1. Canoeing

2. Bradley Wiggins

3. Show jumping

4. Dallas Cowboys

5. Substitute

6. Debut

7. Sprinter

8. Uneven bars

9. Offside trap

10. McLaren

# Game 11 Answers

**One-Minute Round**
1. Preston North End; 2. 12 Rounds in Men's Professional Boxing; 3. Grand National; 4. Athletics; 5. 2010; 6. 147; 7. Sweden; 8. Moana MOO-Caille, Demba BA, NEY Lopez

**Mystery Guest**
Muhammad Ali, Katherine Grainger

**Home or Away**
1. Football. Peter Shilton
2. Rugby League. Andy Farrell

1. Golf. Presidents Cup
2. The Olympics. Cathy Freeman

1. Rugby Union. Stephen Donald
2. Swimming. Karen Pickering

1. Tennis. Caroline Wozniacki
2. Boxing. Sugar Ray Leonard

**Top Ten**
Derbyshire
Gloucestershire
Hampshire
Lancashire
Leicestershire
Northamptonshire
Nottinghamshire
Warwickshire
Worcestershire
Yorkshire

**Buzzer Round**
1. Munich; 2. Benetton; 3. Cycling; 4. 1988; 5. Bernhard Langer; 6. Tottenham Hotspur; 7. Long jump; 8. Dallas Mavericks; 9. Calgary; 10. Hockey

# Game 12

# One-Minute Round

1.  Which cricket team play their home games at Trent Bridge?

2.  Can you solve this sporting equation? '18H on a GC'

3.  In which sport would you hear the words 'backboard' and 'double dribble'?

4.  'ELLEN WON SIX' is an anagram of which person?

5.  In which year did the England football team beat Germany 5-1 away when Sven-Göran Eriksson was manager?

6.  How many Olympic gold medals did Usain Bolt win?

7.  Gustavo Kuerten and Marta have both played internationally for which country?

8.  These three sports stars all share parts of their names with words that can follow sun...

    Lee ? (Rugby Union)
    Joe ? (Athletics)
    Christian ? (Darts)

# Mystery Guest

**In this round you are given three clues
to a sports star's identity.**

### *Who is this Mystery Guest?*

1. I made my Formula One debut in 2007, winning four Grand Prix races in my first season.

2. In 2008, I pipped Felipe Massa to the World title by one point by overtaking Timo Glock in the final stages of the last race of the season.

3. I have the most Grand Prix wins of any British driver in Formula One history.

### *Who is this Mystery Guest?*

1. I was the first winner of the Premier League in my sport.

2. I mentored fellow World Champion Adrian Lewis during his career.

3. I have won a record 16 world titles in my sport.

# Home or Away

In this round there is a choice of a home question for one point or an away question for two.

*Do you want a home question on Football for one point or an away question on Cycling for two?*

1. **Football.** Who, from 2016, won the title in his first two Premier League seasons, doing so with two different clubs?

2. **Cycling.** In 2018, in what cycling event did Rachel Atherton win her fifth World Championship?

*Do you want a home question on Rugby Union for one point or an away question on the Winter Olympics for two?*

1. **Rugby Union.** Which World Cup winner in 2003 won a record 114 caps for his country over a 14-year career?

2. **Winter Olympics.** In 2014, who became the first British woman to win an Olympic medal on the snow?

*Do you want a home question on Golf for one point or an away question on Snooker for two?*

1. **Golf.** In 2010, Colin Montgomerie captained Europe to victory in the Ryder Cup on what course?

2. **Snooker.** Jimmy White lost to Stephen Hendry four times in the 1990s; which fellow Englishman did he lose to in 1991?

*Do you want a home question on Cricket for one point or an away question on American Football for two?*

1. **Cricket.** In 2004, who became the first Englishman to take 200 wickets in One Day Internationals?

2. **American Football.** In 2020, which team won their first Super Bowl in 50 years by defeating the San Francisco 49ers?

# Top Ten

**Name the ten events that make up
an Olympic Decathlon?**

There's a point for each one you correctly identify, but guess one
wrong and you lose your points from this round…

1 .................................................................

2 .................................................................

3 .................................................................

4 .................................................................

5 .................................................................

6 .................................................................

7 .................................................................

8 .................................................................

9 .................................................................

10 ................................................................

# Buzzer Round

**All the questions in this round are about the colour black
or have black in the question or answer...**

1. The All Blacks beat which country in the third place playoff at the
   2019 Rugby World Cup?

2. Which British athlete won Olympic 400m silver in 1996 behind
   Michael Johnson?

3. In snooker, how many points is the black ball worth?

4. The Chicago Blackhawks won which famous trophy for a sixth
   time in 2015?

5. Black Caviar won the Diamond Jubilee Stakes in 2012 at which
   famous English racecourse?

6. Bloomfield Road is home to which former Premier League
   football club?

7. The 2019 US PGA Championship held at Bethpage Black was won
   for the second consecutive time by which American?

8. How many black rings are there on an Olympic Archery target?

9. Elisabeth Black won Team and All-Around Commonwealth gold in
   2018 for which country?

10. The Oakland Raiders NFL franchise are famous for wearing black
    and which other colour?

# Sprint Finish

**Describe these ten sporting words
and phrases to your team...**

1. Playmaker

2. Snooker cue

3. Drop shot

4. Harlequins

5. Dan Marino

6. Opening ceremony

7. Pitcher

8. Knockout

9. Reverse swing

10. Rugby League

# Game 12 Answers

**One-Minute Round**

1. Nottinghamshire; 2. 18 Holes on a Golf Course; 3. Basketball; 4. Lennox Lewis;
5. 2001; 6. Eight; 7. Brazil; 8. Lee BYRNE, Joe DIAL, Christian KIST

**Mystery Guest**

Lewis Hamilton, Phil Taylor

**Home or Away**

1. Football. N'Golo Kanté
2. Cycling. Downhill Mountain Biking

1. Rugby Union. Jason Leonard
2. Winter Olympics. Jenny Jones

1. Golf. Celtic Manor
2. Snooker. John Parrott

1. Cricket. Darren Gough
2. American Football. Kansas City Chiefs

**Top Ten**

100m
Long jump
Shot put
High jump
400m
110m hurdles
Discus
Pole vault
Javelin
1500m

**Buzzer Round**

1. Wales; 2. Roger Black; 3. Seven; 4. Stanley Cup; 5. Ascot; 6. Blackpool;
7. Brooks Koepka; 8. Two; 9. Canada; 10. Silver

# Game 13

# One-Minute Round

1. Which American Football team play their home games at Soldier Field?

2. Can you solve this sporting equation? '5P for the B in S'

3. In which sport would you find a 'sleeper' and a 'turkey'?

4. 'AGELESS EXES' is an anagram of which cricket team?

5. In which year did Bradley Wiggins win the Tour de France?

6. How many players are there on a water polo team?

7. Victor Matfield and Herschelle Gibbs have both played internationally for which country?

8. These three sports stars all share parts of their names with things you associate with romance...

   Joe **?** (Football)
   **?** Brin (Boxing)
   Kevin **?** (Basketball)

# Mystery Guest

**In this round you are given three clues
to a sports star's identity.**

### *Who is this Mystery Guest?*

1. I was born on 17 February 1989 in Mansfield, Nottinghamshire.

2. I was the youngest female to win an individual medal for Great
   Britain at the 2008 Olympics, aged 19.

3. I won double Olympic swimming gold in Beijing and won two
   bronzes four years later.

### *Who is this Mystery Guest?*

1. I won my last Snooker World Championship title in 1999.

2. I beat Jimmy White in all four of our World Championship finals.

3. I won the World Championships a record seven times, before retiring
   in 2012.

# Home or Away

**In this round there is a choice of a home question
for one point or an away question for two.**

*Do you want a home question on Rugby Union for one point or an
away question on Ice Hockey for two?*

1. **Rugby Union.** Which forward has captained his country over 50
   times in the Six Nations but only been on the winning side on six
   occasions in that time?

2. **Ice Hockey.** Which Canadian ice hockey player was credited with
   61 NHL records during his 20-year career?

*Do you want a home question on Football for one point or an
away question on the Olympics for two?*

1. **Football.** Who is the only player to score 100 Premier League goals
   for two different clubs?

2. **The Olympics.** Which sport made its debut at the 2016 Rio
   Olympics, with the two gold medals being won by Australia and Fiji?

*Do you want a home question on Tennis for one point or an away question on MotoGP for two?*

1. **Tennis.** Which British Wheelchair Tennis player won four consecutive Wimbledon doubles titles between 2014 and 2017, partnering Yui Kamiji on each occasion?

2. **MotoGP.** Since 2010, the MotoGP World title has been won by Spaniards Jorge Lorenzo and Marc Márquez on all but one occasion. Which Australian won it that year?

*Do you want a home question on Cricket for one point or an away question on Netball for two?*

1. **Cricket.** Who scored 333 against India in 1990, the highest score by an Englishman in Tests for over 50 years?

2. **Netball.** In which English city did New Zealand win their fifth World Cup title in 2019?

# Top Ten

**Name the ten courses that have hosted golf's
Open Championship since 2000.**

There's a point for each one you correctly identify, but guess one
wrong and you lose your points from this round...

1 .................................................................................

2 .................................................................................

3 .................................................................................

4 .................................................................................

5 .................................................................................

6 .................................................................................

7 .................................................................................

8 .................................................................................

9 .................................................................................

10 ...............................................................................

# Buzzer Round

**All the questions in this round are about the Winter Olympics...**

1. Which city is due to host the 2022 Winter Olympics?

2. Which Scottish woman skipped Great Britain to curling gold in 2002?

3. In which Winter Olympic event do competitors race lying down, feet first on a sled?

4. Which country has won the most ice hockey medals at the Winter Olympics?

5. Which British woman retained her Olympic skeleton title in PyeongChang?

6. In which sport did the Netherlands top the medal table at the 2018 Games?

7. Which Italian skier won five Winter Olympic medals between 1988 and 1994, three of them gold?

8. In what year did Jayne Torvill and Christopher Dean win ice dancing Olympic gold?

9. The Nordic combined consists of cross-country skiing and which other event?

10. Marit Bjørgen, winner of 15 cross-country skiing Olympic medals, is from which country?

# Sprint Finish

**Describe these ten sporting words
and phrases to your team...**

1.  Podium finish

2.  Warming up

3.  Set piece

4.  Claret jug

5.  Peter Crouch

6.  Slam dunk

7.  Murrayfield

8.  Squash

9.  Rallying

10. Flag bearer

# Game 13 Answers

**One-Minute Round**

1. Chicago Bears; 2. 5 Points for the Blue in Snooker; 3. Ten-pin bowling;
4. Essex Eagles; 5. 2012; 6. Seven; 7. South Africa; 8. Joe HART, ROMEO Brin,
Kevin LOVE

**Mystery Guest**

Rebecca Adlington, Stephen Hendry

**Home or Away**

1. Rugby Union. Sergio Parisse
2. Ice Hockey. Wayne Gretzky

1. Football. Alan Shearer
2. The Olympics. Rugby Sevens

1. Tennis. Jordanne Whiley
2. MotoGP. Casey Stoner

1. Cricket. Graham Gooch
2. Netball. Liverpool

**Top Ten**

Royal Portrush
Carnoustie
Royal Birkdale
Royal Troon
St. Andrews
Royal Liverpool (accept Hoylake)
Muirfield
Royal Lytham & St Annes
Royal St George's (accept Sandwich)
Turnberry

**Buzzer Round**

1. Beijing; 2. Rhona Martin; 3. Luge; 4. Canada; 5. Lizzy Yarnold;
6. Speed Skating; 7. Alberto Tomba; 8. 1984; 9. Ski jumping; 10. Norway

# Game 14

# One-Minute Round

1. Which Rugby Union team play their home games at the Madejski Stadium?

2. Can you solve this sporting equation? '4OGM in S for BA'

3. In which sport would you play for the Laver Cup?

4. 'HYPHENED RENTS' is an anagram of which snooker player?

5. In which year did Kelly Holmes win double Olympic gold?

6. To the nearest mile how many miles are there in a marathon?

7. Inge de Bruijn and Wesley Sneijder have both competed internationally for which country?

8. These three sports stars all share parts of their names with things you might spread on toast...

   **?** Handy (Swimming)
   Isaac **?** (Football)
   **?** Bishop (Cricket)

# Mystery Guest

**In this round you are given three clues
to a sports star's identity.**

### Who is this Mystery Guest?

1. I was born in 1986 in Jamaica and my middle name is 'St Leo'.

2. In 2018, I scored twice for Australian soccer team Central Coast Mariners.

3. I'm an eight-time Olympic champion sprinter.

### Who is this Mystery Guest?

1. I hold the record for the most Test catches by an Englishman.

2. I scored a century on my Test debut against India in 2006.

3. In 2015, I surpassed Graham Gooch as England's all-time leading run-scorer in Test matches.

# Home or Away

**In this round there is a choice of a home question for one point or an away question for two.**

*Do you want a home question on Football for one point or an away question on Gymnastics for two?*

1. **Football.** Which club that spent 13 consecutive seasons in the Premier League from 2001 lost to Atlético Madrid in the Europa League Final in 2010?

2. **Gymnastics.** Which sisters have both won European gymnastic gold medals for Great Britain?

*Do you want a home question on Golf for one point or an away question on Formula One for two?*

1. **Golf.** Who captained Europe to victory in Medinah when they won the 2012 Ryder Cup, following a dramatic final day of singles matches?

2. **Formula One.** Which driver holds the record for the most races started in Formula One without winning the World Championship?

*Do you want a home question on Athletics for one point or an away question on Boxing for two?*

1. **Athletics.** In 2005, which city became the first to host the World Athletics Championships on more than one occasion, having hosted the first edition?

2. **Boxing.** Which British boxer won Olympic gold in London and, in 2016, beat Charles Martin to become a World Heavyweight Champion?

*Do you want a home question on Cricket for one point or an away question on British Sport for two?*

1. **Cricket.** Who in 2001, dismissed Jacques Kallis in Trinidad to become the first bowler to take 500 Test wickets?

2. **British Sport.** Leicester Riders beat the London City Royals in the final to be crowned British Champions for a fifth time in which sport?

# Top Ten

**Name the ten horses that won the
Grand National at Aintree in the 1980s.**

There's a point for each one you correctly identify, but guess one
wrong and you lose your points from this round...

1 .......................................................................................

2 .......................................................................................

3 .......................................................................................

4 .......................................................................................

5 .......................................................................................

6 .......................................................................................

7 .......................................................................................

8 .......................................................................................

9 .......................................................................................

10 .......................................................................................

# Buzzer Round

**The answers to all the questions in this round begin
with the letter D. In the case of a person it's the
surname that will begin with that letter...**

1.  In cricket, what word describes a ball off which zero runs are scored?

2.  Which country does Formula One driver Kevin Magnussen represent?

3.  Which American tennis player won the 1999 Wimbledon Ladies' Singles title?

4.  Which shooting event was part of the Olympic programme from 1996 to 2016?

5.  Which football team recorded the lowest ever total of points in a Premier League season with just 11?

6.  In 2001, who became the first male golfer with an alliterative name for over 50 years to win the Open Championship?

7.  What is the name of the Pro 14 Rugby Union team that are based in Newport, Wales?

8.  Who partnered Daniel Goodfellow to 10m Synchro gold at the Rio Olympics?

9. In American Football, what is the name given to the annual player selection process where picks are based on the standings from the previous season?

10. Olympic champion athlete Félix Sánchez won gold for which Caribbean country?

# Sprint Finish

**Describe these ten sporting words
and phrases to your team...**

1. Pitch and putt

2. Javelin

3. World champion

4. Silverstone

5. Andre Agassi

6. Short leg

7. West Ham United

8. Line out

9. Super Bowl

10. Weightlifting

# Game 14 Answers

**One-Minute Round**
1. London Irish; 2. 4 Olympic Gold Medals in Sailing for Ben Ainslie; 3. Tennis;
4. Stephen Hendry; 5. 2004; 6. 26; 7. Netherlands; 8. JAM Handy, Isaac HONEY,
MARGE Bishop

**Mystery Guest**
Usain Bolt, Alastair Cook

**Home or Away**
1. Football. Fulham
2. Gymnastics. Downie Sisters (Beckie and Ellie)

1. Golf. José María Olazábal
2. Formula One. Rubens Barrichello

1. Athletics. Helsinki
2. Boxing. Anthony Joshua

1. Cricket. Courtney Walsh
2. British Sport. Basketball

**Top Ten**
Ben Nevis
Aldaniti
Grittar
Corbiere
Hallo Dandy
Last Suspect
West Tip
Maori Venture
Rhyme 'N' Reason
Little Polveir

**Buzzer Round**
1. Dot; 2. Denmark; 3. Lindsay Davenport; 4. Double trap; 5. Derby County;
6. David Duval; 7. Dragons; 8. Tom Daley; 9. Draft; 10. Dominican Republic

# Game 15

# One-Minute Round

1. Which Rugby Union team play their home games at the Recreation Ground?

2. Can you solve this sporting equation? '7E in the H'

3. In which sport do teams compete in the 'Magic Weekend' every year?

4. 'CHEMICALS HEAR MUCH' is an anagram of which Formula One driver?

5. In which year was the 'Grand National that never was'?

6. What is the maximum amount any player can score with three darts?

7. Lilian Thuram and Mary Pierce have both competed internationally for which country?

8. These three sports stars all share parts of their names with members of the family...

   Kirk **?** (American Football)
   Dean **?** (Rugby Union)
   Ted **?** (Football)

# Mystery Guest

**In this round you are given three clues
to a sports star's identity.**

*Who is this Mystery Guest?*

1. In 1997, I reached all four Grand Slam singles finals, winning three of them.

2. I was Switzerland's first winner of a singles Grand Slam in the open era.

3. In 2017, I partnered Jamie Murray to victory at Wimbledon and the US Open.

*Who is this Mystery Guest?*

1. In 2016, I became Osprey's top try-scoring forward of all time.

2. In 2013, I led the Lions to victory in the deciding Test after injury had ruled out Sam Warburton.

3. I captained Wales to the Grand Slam in the 2019 Six Nations.

# Home or Away

In this round there is a choice of a home question
for one point or an away question for two.

*Do you want a home question on Golf for one point or an away
question on Rugby League for two?*

1.  **Golf.** As of 2019, which golfer won his only major to date at the 2003
    US Open, and was the losing captain at the 2018 Ryder Cup?

2.  **Rugby League.** In which decade did the first Rugby League World
    Cup take place?

*Do you want a home question on Cricket for one point or an away
question on the Olympics for two?*

1.  **Cricket.** In 2003, who became the first player to record hundreds
    against all 18 counties by scoring a century against his former club,
    Middlesex?

2.  **Olympics.** In which sport did Jade Jones win Olympic gold in 2012
    and retain her title four years later?

*Do you want a home question on Football for one point or an away question on Snooker for two?*

1. **Football.** Which country has appeared in all but three of the eight FIFA Women's World Cup Finals, winning it on four occasions?

2. **Snooker.** In 2019, Ding Junhui won which of Snooker's Triple Crown events for a third time, ten years after he last won the title?

*Do you want a home question on Rugby Union for one point or an away question on Motor Sport for two?*

1. **Rugby Union.** In 2001, which Irish player became the first hooker to be named IRB World Player of the Year?

2. **Motor Sport.** In 1995, which British driver became the youngest person to win the World Rally Championship?

# Top Ten

**Name the first ten English teams to play in the group stages of the men's UEFA Champions League.**

There's a point for each one you correctly identify, but guess one wrong and you lose your points from this round...

1  ......................................................................

2  ......................................................................

3  ......................................................................

4  ......................................................................

5  ......................................................................

6  ......................................................................

7  ......................................................................

8  ......................................................................

9  ......................................................................

10  ....................................................................

# Buzzer Round

**All the questions or answers in this
round are about animals...**

1. In cricket, if a batman has been dismissed for zero runs, they are said to be out for a what?

2. The South Africa Rugby Union side are known by what nickname?

3. 'Eddie the Eagle' became the first man since 1928 to represent Great Britain in which Winter Olympic event?

4. Which Italian football club's crest displays three wolves on a yellow and maroon background?

5. In which sport did Mardy Fish reach a career-high ranking of seventh in the world?

6. What is the franchise name of the NFL team based in Miami?

7. Red Alligator and Tiger Roll have both won which annual race?

8. Kevin Sinfield won seven Super League titles with which club between 2004 and 2015?

9. American golfer Craig Stadler is affectionately known by what nickname?

10. In which sport would you see a spider used on the baize?

# Sprint Finish

**Describe these ten sporting words
and phrases to your team...**

1. Golf buggy

2. Sweeper

3. Curling

4. Leotard

5. Fastest lap

6. Michael Jordan

7. Juventus

8. Medley

9. Hurdles

10. Serve and volley

# Game 15 Answers

**One-Minute Round**

1. Bath; 2. 7 Events in the Heptathlon; 3. Rugby League; 4. Michael Schumacher;
5. 1993; 6. 180; 7. France; 8. Kirk COUSINS, Dean MUMM, Ted UNKEL

**Mystery Guest**

Martina Hingis, Alun Wyn Jones

**Home or Away**

1. Golf. Jim Furyk
2. Rugby League. 1950s

1. Cricket. Mark Ramprakash
2. Olympics. Taekwondo

1. Football. USA
2. Snooker. UK Championship

1. Rugby Union. Keith Wood
2. Motor Sport. Colin McRae

**Top Ten**

Arsenal
Blackburn Rovers
Chelsea
Leeds United
Leicester City
Liverpool
Manchester City
Manchester United
Newcastle United
Tottenham Hotpsur

**Buzzer Round**

1. Duck; 2. Springboks; 3. Ski jumping; 4. AS Roma; 5. Tennis; 6. Dolphins;
7. Grand National; 8. Leeds Rhinos; 9. Walrus; 10. Snooker

# Game 16

# One-Minute Round

1. Which NFL team play their home games at Candlestick Park?

2. Can you solve this sporting equation? '6B in an O'

3. What fruit is carved onto the top of the men's Wimbledon trophy?

4. 'MISSILE BONE' is an anagram of which Olympic champion?

5. In which year did Damon Hill win the Formula One World Championship?

6. What number comes between 20 and 18 on a standard dartboard?

7. Søren Hansen and Ebbe Sand have both represented which country?

8. These three sports stars all share parts of their names with types of music...

   **?** Carlin (Swimming)
   Robert **?** (Golf)
   Alexander **?** (Tennis)

# Mystery Guest

**In this round you are given three clues
to a sports star's identity.**

### *Who is this Mystery Guest?*

1.  In 2012, I became the youngest multiple major winner since Seve Ballesteros.

2.  I became the second golfer ever to have won the Silver Medal at the Open and the Open Championship itself.

3.  I have won the Ryder Cup with Europe on four occasions.

### *Who is this Mystery Guest?*

1.  I was born in Italy and followed my father's footsteps into the same sport as him.

2.  I won my seven World Championships between 2001 and 2009.

3.  I won most of my titles riding for Yamaha.

# Home or Away

In this round there is a choice of a home question
for one point or an away question for two.

*Do you want a home question on Tennis for one point or an away
question on the Winter Olympics for two?*

1. **Tennis.** Which American tennis player and former US Open
   champion is the main court at Flushing Meadows named after?

2. **Winter Olympics.** In which sport have Alberto Tomba and Julia
   Mancuso both been Winter Olympic champions?

*Do you want a home question on Rugby Union for one point or an
away question on the Paralympics for two?*

1. **Rugby Union.** Which scrum half scored his first international test
   try for the Lions in 1997, before scoring his first try for his country
   eight months later?

2. **Paralympics.** Who won five swimming gold medals at the
   Paralympics in the 1990s, before going onto win nine cycling gold
   medals later in her career?

*Do you want a home question on Cricket for one point or an away question on Formula One for two?*

1.  **Cricket.** Which county have won a record number of County Championships, which included back-to-back titles in 2014 and 2015?

2.  **Formula One.** In 2015, who became the youngest driver to score points in a Formula One Grand Prix?

*Do you want a home question on Football for one point or an away question on Horse Racing for two?*

1.  **Football.** Since 2000, which manager has won league titles in four different countries, as well as the Champions League in 2004 and 2010?

2.  **Horse Racing.** Who rode Fujiyama Crest to victory at Ascot in September 1996 to become the first jockey to win all seven races on the card at a single meeting?

# Top Ten

**Name the top ten countries in the medal table
at the 2016 Summer Olympics.**

There's a point for each one you correctly identify, but guess one
wrong and you lose your points from this round...

1 ..........................................................................

2 ..........................................................................

3 ..........................................................................

4 ..........................................................................

5 ..........................................................................

6 ..........................................................................

7 ..........................................................................

8 ..........................................................................

9 ..........................................................................

10 .........................................................................

# Buzzer Round

**All the questions in this round are about the colour green
or have green in the question or answer...**

1.  Which American became the first golfer to win six Green Jackets at
    the US Masters?

2.  How many points is the green ball worth in snooker?

3.  Which England international won 12 caps and played in goal for
    West Ham between 2006 and 2012?

4.  What is the name of the caps worn by the Australian cricket team?

5.  For which American Football team have Brett Favre and Aaron
    Rodgers played quarterback?

6.  Sprinter Maurice Greene won two Olympic gold medals in
    which city?

7.  In which sport is the green jersey awarded to the top sprinter?

8.  In crown green bowls, the target for bowlers is known as the what?

9.  Which 2003 World Cup-winning centre scored 31 tries for England?

10. On a standard dartboard how many scoring sections are green?

# Sprint Finish

**Describe these ten sporting words
and phrases to your team...**

1. Discus

2. Lionel Messi

3. Yorker

4. Skeleton

5. Triple jump

6. Boston Celtics

7. Australian Open

8. Driving range

9. World record

10. Undercard

# Game 16 Answers

**One-Minute Round**
1. San Francisco 49ers; 2. 6 Balls in an Over; 3. Pineapple; 4. Simone Biles; 5. 1996; 6. One; 7. Denmark; 8. JAZZ Carlin, Robert ROCK, Alexander POPP

**Mystery Guest**
Rory McIlroy, Valentino Rossi

**Home or Away**
1. Tennis. Arthur Ashe
2. Winter Olympics. Alpine Skiing

1. Rugby Union. Matt Dawson
2. Paralympics. Sarah Storey

1. Cricket. Yorkshire
2. Formula One. Max Verstappen

1. Football. José Mourinho
2. Horse Racing. Frankie Dettori

**Top Ten**
USA
Great Britain
China
Russia
Germany
Japan
France
South Korea
Italy
Australia

**Buzzer Round**
1. Jack Nicklaus; 2. Three; 3. Robert Green; 4. Baggy Greens; 5. Green Bay Packers; 6. Sydney; 7. Cycling; 8. Jack; 9. Will Greenwood; 10. 21

# Game 17

# One-Minute Round

1. Which football team play their home games at Pittodrie?

2. Can you solve this sporting equation? '3P for a DG in RU'

3. In which sport is the Thomas Cup contested?

4. 'SHY CHOIR' is an anagram of which Olympic champion?

5. In which year did Maria Sharapova win the Ladies' Singles title at Wimbledon?

6. How many times have the USA hosted the Winter Olympics?

7. Vivian Cheruiyot and Steve Tikolo have both represented which country?

8. These three sports stars all share parts of their names with things you might find on a bicycle…

   Hank **?** (American Football)
   Greg **?** (Baseball)
   Ian **?** (Cricket)

# Mystery Guest

**In this round you are given three clues
to a sports star's identity.**

### Who is this Mystery Guest?

1. I was born in Harlow, Essex in 1992.

2. I married a fellow British Olympic cyclist in 2016.

3. As of 2020, I am the most successful British female Olympian.

### Who is this Mystery Guest?

1. I am the youngest goal scorer in World Cup history.

2. I starred in the 1981 film *Escape to Victory* alongside Sylvester Stallone and Michael Caine.

3. I played in the World Cup Final three times for my country.

# Home or Away

**In this round there is a choice of a home question
for one point or an away question for two.**

*Do you want a home question on Cricket for one point or an away
question on Boxing for two?*

1.  **Cricket.** In 2016, West Indian batsman Carlos Brathwaite hit which
    England bowler for four consecutive sixes in the final over, to help
    his country win the World Twenty20 competition?

2.  **Boxing.** Which boxer, nicknamed 'Real Deal', is the only man
    to have won the Heavyweight World Championship on four
    separate occasions?

*Do you want a home question on Rugby Union for one point or an
away question on Gymnastics for two?*

1.  **Rugby Union.** Which Irishman won a record 17 caps for the British
    and Irish Lions across five tours from 1962 to 1974?

2.  **Gymnastics.** Which 16-year-old Englishwoman won four
    Commonwealth gold medals in 2014?

*Do you want a home question on Football for one point or an away question on Rugby League for two?*

1.  **Football.** In 2019, who won his second Premier League title and in the same year won the Africa Cup of Nations with his country?

2.  **Rugby League.** Which country reached the semi-finals at the last three World Cups but have failed to make the final in any of them?

*Do you want a home question on Golf for one point or an away question on Snooker for two?*

1.  **Golf.** Who in 2007 became the first South American to win one of Golf's majors for over 40 years by winning the US Open at Oakmont?

2.  **Snooker.** Which Snooker player ended Stephen Hendry's five-year unbeaten streak at the Masters in 1994, in an all-Scottish encounter?

# Top Ten

**Name the ten men that won the most tennis
Grand Slam Singles titles between 1980 and 2019.**

There's a point for each one you correctly identify, but guess one
wrong and you lose your points from this round...

1  ................................................................

2  ................................................................

3  ................................................................

4  ................................................................

5  ................................................................

6  ................................................................

7  ................................................................

8  ................................................................

9  ................................................................

10  ................................................................

# Buzzer Round

**All the questions in this round are about Europe
and sports stars from that continent…**

1. In 2017, which European country was granted Test cricket status for the first time?

2. In 2016, which Dutch city hosted a round of the Premier League Darts for the first time?

3. Young Boys and Grasshopper Club have both won the domestic football league in which country?

4. Athlete Jo Pavey is a European Champion over what distance?

5. Which country has provided the most finalists in the European Rugby Champions Cup?

6. Which British circuit hosted Formula One's European Grand Prix the first time it was held in the country in 1983?

7. In golf, which Swedish woman won ten majors between 1995 and 2006?

8. Luca Brecel is the first snooker player from which country to appear at the World Championships?

9. What nationality is Wimbledon tennis champion Petra Kvitová?

10. The prestigious Group One race the Prix de l'Arc de Triomphe is held annually at which European racecourse in October?

# Sprint Finish

**Describe these ten sporting words
and phrases to your team...**

1. Archery

2. Freestyle

3. Zlatan Ibrahimović

4. Celtic Manor

5. Puck

6. Wigan Warriors

7. Coach

8. Pit Lane

9. Karate

10. Hall of Fame

# Game 17 Answers

**One-Minute Round**

1. Aberdeen; 2. 3 Points for a Drop Goal in Rugby Union; 3. Badminton; 4. Chris Hoy; 5. 2004; 6. Four; 7. Kenya; 8. Hank BASKETT, Greg BRAKE, Ian BELL

**Mystery Guest**

Laura Kenny, Pelé

**Home or Away**

1. Cricket. Ben Stokes
2. Boxing. Evander Holyfield

1. Rugby Union. Willie John McBride
2. Gymnastics. Claudia Fragapane

1. Football. Riyad Mahrez
2. Rugby League. Fiji

1. Golf. Angel Cabrera
2. Snooker. Alan McManus

**Top Ten**

Roger Federer
Rafael Nadal
Novak Djokovic
Pete Sampras
Andre Agassi
Ivan Lendl
Mats Wilander
Stefan Edberg
Boris Becker
John McEnroe

**Buzzer Round**

1. Ireland; 2. Rotterdam; 3. Switzerland; 4. 10,000m; 5. France; 6. Brands Hatch; 7. Annika Sörenstam; 8. Belgium; 9. Czech; 10. Longchamp

# Game 18

# One-Minute Round

1. Which cricket team play their home games at Grace Road?

2. Can you solve this sporting equation? '5SWC for RO'

3. In which sport would you use a flight at the oche?

4. 'CHAIRMAN UNTESTED' is an anagram of which football team?

5. In which year was the first World Athletics Championship held?

6. How many fences are jumped in the Grand National?

7. Agnieszka Radwańska and Robert Lewandowski have both represented which country?

8. These three sports stars all share parts of their names with places you can grow food...

   Michael ? (Baseball)
   Paul ? (Bobsleigh)
   Nate ? (American Football)

# Mystery Guest

**In this round you are given three clues
to a sports star's identity.**

## Who is this Mystery Guest?

1. I made my professional Rugby Union debut for Saracens in 2008 at the age of 17.

2. My father is a former Rugby League international.

3. I was England's top points scorer in the 2019 Rugby Union World Cup.

## Who is this Mystery Guest?

1. I was born in 1973 in Cheshire, England.

2. I won World Athletics Championship gold in 2005 in Helsinki.

3. I held the record for fastest female marathon runner between 2002 and 2019.

# Home or Away

**In this round there is a choice of a home question for one point or an away question for two.**

*Do you want a home question on Football for one point or an away question on Darts for two?*

1. **Football.** Which Italian team did Diego Maradona help to win the Serie A title for the first time in their history in 1987?

2. **Darts.** Who beat Michael van Gerwen to win his first PDC World Championship in 2020, six years after being beaten by the same player in his only previous final?

*Do you want a home question on Rugby Union for one point or an away question on Formula One for two?*

1. **Rugby Union.** Which player scored a record 64 tries in 101 tests for Australia between 1982 and 1996?

2. **Formula One.** Which Formula One World Champion won his 21st Grand Prix in 2018 for Ferrari, having won his 20th with Lotus in 2013?

*Do you want a home question on Golf for one point or an away question on American Football for two?*

1. **Golf.** Paul Lawrie, Tom Lehman and Justin Leonard all won their only Major Championship at which tournament?

2. **American Football.** Which team reached four consecutive Super Bowls at the start of the 1990s, without winning any of them?

*Do you want a home question on Cricket for one point or an away question on Horse Racing for two?*

1. **Cricket.** In 2017, which Indian spinner became the fastest to take 300 Test wickets, overtaking Dennis Lille's record?

2. **Horse Racing.** Jim Culloty rode Best Mate to three consecutive wins in which famous annual race between 2002 and 2004?

# Top Ten

**Name the ten sports that England won the
most medals in at the 2018 Commonwealth Games.**

There's a point for each one you correctly identify, but guess one
wrong and you lose your points from this round...

1 ..................................................................

2 ..................................................................

3 ..................................................................

4 ..................................................................

5 ..................................................................

6 ..................................................................

7 ..................................................................

8 ..................................................................

9 ..................................................................

10 ..................................................................

# Buzzer Round

**All the questions in this round are to
do with close finishes in sport...**

1. Japan beat South Africa at the 2015 Rugby World Cup thanks to a winning try in the 84th minute. Who was their coach?

2. Ole Gunnar Solskjær scored the winning goal in the 1999 Champions League Final in which stadium?

3. Martin Kaymer sealed the 2012 Ryder Cup for Europe with a five-foot putt on the 18th green at which golf club?

4. Neptune Collonges won which famous horse race in 2012 in a photo finish?

5. The 2019 Cricket World Cup Final was decided in a Super Over, Trent Boult and which other player bowled them?

6. In what year did Lewis Hamilton win the Formula One World Championship on the final lap at the Brazil Grand Prix?

7. Who won the 2019 Wimbledon final on a tiebreak after an epic battle lasting nearly five hours with Roger Federer?

8. Who won the 1985 World Snooker Championship Final on the final ball of the final frame?

9. Michael Phelps won one of his gold medals in Beijing by 0.01 of a second in the 100m Butterfly. How many gold medals did he win at those games?

10. Who scored an injury-time winner for Manchester City as they won the 2012 Premier League title in the last game of the season?

# Sprint Finish

**Describe these ten sporting words
and phrases to your team...**

1.  Jonny Wilkinson

2.  Goalmouth scramble

3.  Home straight

4.  Anfield

5.  Boat Race

6.  Stuart Broad

7.  Ace

8.  Spider

9.  Gold medal

10. Unforced error

# Game 18 Answers

**One-Minute Round**

1. Leicestershire; 2. 5 Snooker World Championships for Ronnie O'Sullivan;
3. Darts; 4. Manchester United; 5. 1983; 6. 30; 7. Poland;
8. Michael GREENHOUSE, Paul FIELD, Nate ORCHARD

**Mystery Guest**

Owen Farrell, Paula Radcliffe

**Home or Away**

1. Football. Napoli
2. Darts. Peter Wright

1. Rugby Union. David Campese
2. Formula One. Kimi Räikkönen

1. Golf. Open Championship
2. American Football. Buffalo Bills

1. Cricket. Ravi Ashwin
2. Horse Racing. Cheltenham Gold Cup

**Top Ten**

Swimming
Athletics
Gymnastics
Cycling
Boxing
Diving
Shooting
Badminton
Table Tennis
Weightlifting

**Buzzer Round**

1. Eddie Jones; 2. Nou Camp; 3. Medinah; 4. Grand National; 5. Jofra Archer;
6. 2008; 7. Novak Djokovic; 8. Dennis Taylor; 9. Eight; 10. Sergio Agüero

# Game 19

# One-Minute Round

1.  Which football team play their home games at Ashton Gate?

2.  Can you solve this sporting equation? '4Q in a G of AF'

3.  In which of golf's majors is the winner awarded the Wanamaker trophy?

4.  'TRIP A HOLLY' is an anagram of which multiple world champion?

5.  In which year did Jesse Owens win four Olympic gold medals?

6.  How many ends are there in a Women's Olympic curling match?

7.  Blessing Okagbare and Nwankwo Kanu have both represented which country?

8.  These three sports stars all share parts of their names with things you might find in a book...

    Derrick **?** (Basketball)
    Steve **?** (Baseball)
    Mick **?** (Boxing)

# Mystery Guest

**In this round you are given three clues
to a sports star's identity.**

### Who is this Mystery Guest?

1. In 2003 I was drafted with the first pick overall in the NBA.

2. I won the NBA Championship with Miami Heat and the Cleveland Cavaliers.

3. I go by the nickname 'King James'.

### Who is this Mystery Guest?

1. I did a set at Glastonbury in 2016 as DJ Thundermuscle.

2. My defeat to Dennis Taylor holds the record for the UK's largest post-midnight TV audience.

3. In the 1980s, I reached eight World Championship finals.

# Home or Away

In this round there is a choice of a home question
for one point or an away question for two.

*Do you want a home question on Football for one point or an
away question on Motor Racing for two?*

1. **Football.** Which manager reached the Europa League final for
   a fourth time in 2019, winning the first three with the same
   Spanish club?

2. **Motor Racing.** In 2003, Petter Solberg became the first driver from
   which country to win the World Rally Championship?

*Do you want a home question on Rugby Union for one point or an
away question on the Winter Olympics for two?*

1. **Rugby Union.** Which Munster player is the only person to have
   scored over 1,000 points in European Rugby's Champions Cup?

2. **Winter Olympics.** At the Winter Olympics, Nordic-Combined
   sees competitors take part in Cross-Country Skiing and which
   other sport?

*Do you want a home question on Athletics for one point or an away question on Baseball for two?*

1. **Athletics.** In which sport is New Zealand's Valerie Adams a four-time World Champion and a double Olympic gold medallist?

2. **Baseball.** In 2016, which team finally ended a run of 108 years without winning the World Series, by beating the Cleveland Indians?

*Do you want a home question on Cricket for one point or an away question on Swimming for two?*

1. **Cricket.** Which country featured in each of the first three Cricket World Cup Finals, winning two and losing one?

2. **Swimming.** Which English swimmer won Commonwealth gold in 2010 and 2014 in the women's 50m Butterfly?

# Top Ten

**Name the ten Rugby League teams that have reached the Challenge Cup Final on the most occasions.**

There's a point for each one you correctly identify, but guess one wrong and you lose your points from this round…

1 ..................................................................

2 ..................................................................

3 ..................................................................

4 ..................................................................

5 ..................................................................

6 ..................................................................

7 ..................................................................

8 ..................................................................

9 ..................................................................

10 .................................................................

# Buzzer Round

**The answers to all the questions in this round begin
with the letter L. In the case of a person it's the
surname that will begin with that letter...**

1. Which English football team reached the semi-finals of the
   Champions League in 2001?

2. In which sport do players use a stick to carry, pass, catch and
   throw the ball?

3. Who scored one run in a partnership of 76 with Ben Stokes to help
   England win the third Test of the 2019 Ashes?

4. Which Rugby Union team were European Champions four times
   between 2009 and 2018?

5. Which Austrian driver won three Formula One World
   Championships?

6. Which European country won Basketball bronze medals at the 1992,
   1996 and 2000 Summer Olympics?

7. Which Scottish golfer won the 1985 Open Championship and the
   1988 US Masters?

8. What is the franchise name that is shared by an AFL team from
   Brisbane and a NFL team from Detroit?

9. Which British athlete won heptathlon gold at the Sydney Olympics in 2000?

10. Which tennis player is the main arena that hosts the Australian Open named after?

# Sprint Finish

**Describe these ten sporting words
and phrases to your team...**

1. Anthony Joshua

2. Bronze medal

3. Fantasy football

4. Chequered flag

5. Ice hockey

6. Bramall Lane

7. Approach shot

8. Torvill and Dean

9. 100m

10. Home run

# Game 19 Answers

**One-Minute Round**

1. Bristol City; 2. 4 Quarters in a Game of American Football; 3. USPGA; 4. Phil Taylor; 5. 1936; 6. Ten; 7 Nigeria; 8. Derrick CARACTER, Steve CHAPTER, Mick FORWARD

**Mystery Guest**

LeBron James, Steve Davis

**Home or Away**

1. Football. Unai Emery
2. Motor Racing. Norway

1. Rugby Union. Ronan O'Gara
2. Winter Olympics. Ski Jumping

1. Athletics. Shot Put
2. Baseball. Chicago Cubs

1. Cricket. West Indies
2. Swimming. Fran Halsall

**Top Ten**

Wigan Warriors
Leeds Rhinos
St Helens
Warrington Wolves
Hull FC
Widnes Vikings
Halifax
Bradford Bulls
Hudddersfield Giants
Wakefield Trinity

**Buzzer Round**

1. Leeds United; 2. Lacrosse; 3. Jack Leach; 4. Leinster; 5. Niki Lauda;
6. Lithuania; 7. Sandy Lyle; 8. Lions; 9. Denise Lewis; 10. Rod Laver

# Game 20

# One-Minute Round

1. What is the franchise name of the NHL Ice Hockey team from Edmonton?

2. Can you solve this sporting equation? '3 GJ won by NF'

3. In which sport can you win the Lance Todd Trophy?

4. 'ANIMAL WIRELESS' is an anagram of which multiple Grand Slam champion?

5. In which year was the first Rugby Union World Cup held?

6. How many frames need to be won to win the World Snooker Championship Final?

7. Nelson Évora and Nuno Gomes have both represented which country?

8. These three sports stars all share parts of their names with types of bed...

   Robby **?** (Baseball)
   Casten **?** (Rowing)
   Ian **?** (Fencing)

# Mystery Guest

**In this round you are given three clues
to a sports star's identity.**

### *Who is this Mystery Guest?*

1.  I won my first Olympic gold medal in 2016 with a time of
    57.13 seconds.

2.  A year later, I broke two world records in a day at the World
    Championships in Budapest.

3.  At the end of 2019, I held the 50m breaststroke record in a
    lightning-quick 25.95 seconds.

### *Who is this Mystery Guest?*

1.  I'm a major-winning golfer and I was born in Johannesburg in 1980.

2.  I won the silver medal at the Open Championship in 1998.

3.  I won Olympic gold for Great Britain in Rio in the men's
    individual tournament.

# Home or Away

**In this round there is a choice of a home question
for one point or an away question for two.**

*Do you want a home question on Football for one point or an
away question on the Winter Olympics for two?*

1. **Football.** Which Dutchman won the Premier League Golden
   Boot in 2012 with one club and again the following year with
   another team?

2. **Winter Olympics.** In 2017, who became the first British woman to
   win World Championship Short Track Speed Skating gold?

*Do you want a home question on Rugby Union for one point or an
away question on Boxing for two?*

1. **Rugby Union.** Which country was the only team to beat hosts
   Japan at the 2019 Rugby World Cup?

2. **Boxing.** Which British boxer lost in his first World title fight
   with Jorge Linares in 2017, five years after winning Olympic
   Bantamweight gold?

*Do you want a home question on Golf for one point or an away question on Formula One for two?*

1.  **Golf.** There were only two golfers to reach world number one between 2000 and 2009, Tiger Woods and which other player?

2.  **Formula One.** Who, in 1998, became the first Finnish driver since Keke Rosberg to win the Formula One World Championship?

*Do you want a home question on Tennis for one point or an away question on Basketball for two?*

1.  **Tennis.** Which British woman won three Grand Slam singles titles in her career, including the Wimbledon title in 1977?

2.  **Basketball.** Which team have won the NBA Finals six times, with all their victories coming in the 1990s?

# Top Ten

**Bobby Moore captained his country to victory
in the World Cup Final in 1966; who were the
other ten players to feature for England that day?**

There's a point for each one you correctly identify, but guess one
wrong and you lose your points from this round...

1 .................................................................

2 .................................................................

3 .................................................................

4 .................................................................

5 .................................................................

6 .................................................................

7 .................................................................

8 .................................................................

9 .................................................................

10 .................................................................

# Buzzer Round

**All the questions in this round are about people called Chris...**

1.  In which city did Chris Hoy win the first of his six Olympic gold medals?

2.  Who did Chris Evert face in 13 Grand Slam tennis Singles Finals in her career?

3.  In which sport did Chris Mears partner Jack Laugher to Olympic gold?

4.  Which French football team did Chris Waddle play for between 1989 and 1992?

5.  Which West Indian became the first batsman to score a century in each of international cricket's three formats?

6.  Former England Rugby Union captain Chris Robshaw has made over 250 appearances for which club side?

7.  Great Britain's Chris Tomlinson won a bronze medal at the European Athletics Championships in which field event?

8.  Englishman Chris Wood was awarded the Silver Medal in 2008 for finishing as the leading amateur at which of golf's majors?

9.  Who did Chris Eubank beat in November 1990 to become WBO Middleweight Champion of the World for the first time?

10. Chris Walker-Hebborn and Chris Cook are Commonwealth Champions in which sport?

# Sprint Finish

**Describe these ten sporting words
and phrases to your team...**

1.  Colin Jackson

2.  Europa League

3.  Blinkers

4.  Wing defence

5.  Commentator

6.  New balls please

7.  Munster

8.  Ice Skating

9.  Ally Pally

10. Michael Phelps

# **Game 20** Answers

---

**One-Minute Round**

1. Oilers; 2. 3 Green Jackets won by Nick Faldo; 3. Rugby League;
4. Serena Williams; 5. 1987; 6. 18; 7. Portugal; 8. Robby HAMMOCK,
Casten BUNK, Ian SINGLE

**Mystery Guest**

Adam Peaty, Justin Rose

**Home or Away**

1. Football. Robin van Persie
2. Winter Olympics. Elise Christie

1. Rugby Union. South Africa
2. Boxing. Luke Campbell

1. Golf. Vijay Singh
2. Formula One. Mika Häkkinen

1. Tennis. Virginia Wade
2. Basketball. Chicago Bulls

**Top Ten**

Gordon Banks
George Cohen
Jack Charlton
Ray Wilson
Nobby Stiles
Alan Ball
Bobby Charlton
Martin Peters
Geoff Hurst
Roger Hunt

**Buzzer Round**

1. Athens; 2. Martina Navratilova; 3. Diving; 4. Olympique de Marseille;
5. Chris Gayle; 6. Harlequins; 7. Long Jump; 8. Open Championship;
9. Nigel Benn; 10. Swimming

# Game 21

# One-Minute Round

1. What is the franchise name of the NBA basketball team based in Milwaukee?

2. Can you solve this sporting equation? '52L in the BGP'

3. In which Commonwealth sport do competitors target a jack?

4. 'MARRIED LAD' is an anagram of which football team?

5. In which year did England win the Ashes for the first time since 1987?

6. How many teams were there in Rugby League's Super League in 2019?

7. Leander Paes and Ishant Sharma have both represented which country?

8. These three sports stars all share parts of their names with chess pieces...

   Zat **?** (Football)
   Ian **?** (Cricket)
   Mervyn **?** (Darts)

# Mystery Guest

**In this round you are given three clues
to a sports star's identity.**

## Who is this Mystery Guest?

1. I was named as the BBC Overseas Sports Personality of the Year in 1994.

2. In 1990, I made my Test debut for the West Indies.

3. As of the start of 2020, I am the holder of both the record first-class individual innings and the record Test individual innings.

## Who is this Mystery Guest?

1. I won team gold at London 2012 alongside Laura Bechtolsheimer and Carl Hester.

2. I have won four Olympic medals with Valegro.

3. I am Great Britain's most successful Olympic equestrian rider.

# Home or Away

**In this round there is a choice of a home question for one point or an away question for two.**

*Do you want a home question on Football for one point or an away question on Snooker for two?*

1. **Football.** Who is the only goalkeeper to have kept over 200 clean sheets in Premier League history?

2. **Snooker.** Which Englishman lost in his two World Snooker Championship final appearances, in 2008 and 2012, both against Ronnie O'Sullivan?

*Do you want a home question on Golf for one point or an away question on Motor Sports for two?*

1. **Golf.** Who was the only golfer whose surname begins with the letter D to win a major in the 1990s?

2. **Motor Sports.** Between 2000 and 2010, who was the only Englishman to win the Superbike World Championship on more than one occasion?

*Do you want a home question on Tennis for one point or an away question on Boxing for two?*

1. **Tennis.** Which German woman ended Serena Williams' three and a half-year reign as world number one in 2016?

2. **Boxing.** In December 2019, Anthony Joshua beat Andy Ruiz Jr in a Heavyweight rematch, in which Asian country?

*Do you want a home question on Cricket for one point or an away question on Gymnastics for two?*

1. **Cricket.** In 2011, the home ground of which county hosted its first men's Test match?

2. **Gymnastics.** Who became Britain's first female gymnast to win a medal at the European Championships, the World Championships and the Olympics?

# Top Ten

**Other than New Zealand, who are top of the list, name the ten teams that have won the most games at the Rugby Union World Cup.**

There's a point for each one you correctly identify, but guess one wrong and you lose your points from this round...

1 ....................................................................

2 ....................................................................

3 ....................................................................

4 ....................................................................

5 ....................................................................

6 ....................................................................

7 ....................................................................

8 ....................................................................

9 ....................................................................

10 ....................................................................

# Buzzer Round

**All the questions in this round focus
on surprising winners...**

1. Who managed Leicester City when they defied 5,000/1 odds to win the Premier League title in 2016?

2. Which country in 2003 reached the semi-final of the Cricket World Cup for the first time?

3. In which year did the USA beat the Soviet Union in the Lake Placid Winter Olympics in what became known as the Miracle on Ice?

4. In 2015, Tyson Fury became the first man in 11 years to defeat which heavyweight boxer?

5. Which Swedish tennis player in 2009, became the first man to beat Rafael Nadal at the French Open?

6. With Jordan Spieth leading the first three rounds of the 2016 Masters, which Englishman surpassed him on the final day to win the tournament?

7. Swimmer Rebecca Adlington won double Olympic gold as a 19-year-old, in which city?

8. In 2009, which team won the World Championship and the Constructors' Championship, in their first and only season in Formula One?

9. What nationality is speed skater Steven Bradbury, who won Winter Olympic gold after his opponents were involved in a last-corner collision?

10. Which Englishman defeated Phil Taylor in 2018 to win his first PDC World Championship on his debut?

# Sprint Finish

**Describe these ten sporting words
and phrases to your team...**

1. Bundesliga

2. Surfing

3. Pelaton

4. Conversion

5. Simone Biles

6. Hamstring

7. Chicane

8. Dressage

9. Madison Square Garden

10. Shin pads

# Game 21 Answers

**One-Minute Round**
1. Bucks; 2. 52 Laps in the British Grand Prix; 3. Lawn Bowls; 4. Real Madrid;
5. 2005; 6. 12; 7. India; 8. Zat KNIGHT, Ian BISHOP, Mervyn KING

**Mystery Guest**
Brian Lara, Charlotte Dujardin

**Home or Away**
1. Football. Petr Čech
2. Snooker. Ali Carter

1. Golf. John Daly
2. Motor Sports. James Toseland

1. Tennis. Angelique Kerber
2. Boxing. Saudi Arabia

1. Cricket. Hampshire
2. Gymnastics. Beth Tweddle

**Top Ten**
Australia
France
England
South Africa
Wales
Ireland
Scotland
Argentina
Italy
Samoa

**Buzzer Round**
1. Claudio Ranieri; 2. Kenya; 3. 1980; 4. Wladimir Klitschk; 5. Robin Söderling;
6. Danny Willett; 7. Beijing; 8. Brawn; 9. Australian; 10. Rob Cross

# Game 22

# One-Minute Round

1. Which Rugby League team play their home games at the Jungle?

2. Can you solve this sporting equation? '9I in a BG'

3. In which sport do countries compete in the Fed Cup?

4. 'UNREAL YANK' is an anagram of which Olympic champion?

5. In which year did Michael Schumacher win his first Formula One World Title?

6. How many teams played in the first Premier League season?

7. Alexis Sánchez and Fernando González have both represented which country?

8. These three sports stars all share parts of their names with words that can follow LAST...

   Wilfred **?** (Athletics)
   **?** Ruffin (Baseball)
   Jack **?** (Boxing)

# Mystery Guest

**In this round you are given three clues
to a sports star's identity.**

## Who is this Mystery Guest?

1. In 1997, I battled with Donovan Bailey over 150m.

2. I won four Olympic gold medals and eight World Championship golds for the USA.

3. I was well known for my golden shoes, upright running style and deep voice.

## Who is this Mystery Guest?

1. In 2016, I retained my Olympic gold medal for Great Britain.

2. In 2019, I won a tour event for the first time in over two and a half years.

3. In 2015, I defeated David Goffin to help Great Britain win the Davis Cup for the first time since 1936.

# Home or Away

**In this round there is a choice of a home question for one point or an away question for two.**

*Do you want a home question on Football for one point or an away question on Darts for two?*

1. **Football.** In November 2015, which English striker scored in a record 11th consecutive Premier League match?

2. **Darts.** Who lost to his compatriot Jelle Klaasen in the 2006 BDO World Championship Final, before winning the PDC World Championship at the first time of asking a year later?

*Do you want a home question on Tennis for one point or an away question on Horse Racing for two?*

1. **Tennis.** Which country did Justine Henin and Kim Clijsters help to their first Fed Cup title in 2001?

2. **Horse Racing.** Which jockey won the Grand National on Papillon in 2000, and on Hedgehunter five years later?

*Do you want a home question on Rugby Union for one point or an away question on Swimming for two?*

1. **Rugby Union.** Which Frenchman, who won 81 caps at full back, scored the deciding try in the 1987 World Cup semi-final?

2. **Swimming.** By winning eight of them at the Olympics in Beijing, Michael Phelps broke which swimmer's record for most gold medals at a single games?

*Do you want a home question on Cricket for one point or an away question on Sailing for two?*

1. **Cricket.** Which team have never won Cricket's County Championship and since 2010 have finished runners-up five times?

2. **Sailing.** Which sailing race was first competed for in 1851, and will next be contested by Team New Zealand and Luna Rosso?

# Top Ten

**Name the ten British drivers to win the
Formula One World Championship.**

There's a point for each one you correctly identify, but guess one
wrong and you lose your points from this round...

1  .................................................................

2  .................................................................

3  .................................................................

4  .................................................................

5  .................................................................

6  .................................................................

7  .................................................................

8  .................................................................

9  .................................................................

10 .................................................................

# Buzzer Round

**The answers to all the questions in this round begin
with the letter E. In the case of a person, it's the
surname that will begin with that letter...**

1. Great Britain's Charlotte Dujardin is a multiple Olympic champion in which sport?

2. What is the franchise name of the NFL team from Philadelphia?

3. Which tennis player won the last of her 18 Grand Slam singles titles in 1986?

4. In 2015, which Rugby Union team became the first Scottish club to reach a major European final?

5. Which Englishman won the 2002 World Snooker Championship?

6. Which Canadian city hosted the 2001 World Athletics Championships?

7. Which Portugal international won the Ballon d'Or in 1965?

8. Which South African major-winning golfer is nicknamed the 'Big Easy'?

9. Foil, Sabre and which other discipline is there in Olympic fencing?

10. In 2019, which team won cricket's County Championship?

# Sprint Finish

**Describe these ten sporting words
and phrases to your team…**

1. Half time whistle

2. Weigh-in

3. Rally driver

4. Individual pursuit

5. Phil Mickelson

6. Bowler

7. Handball

8. Katherine Grainger

9. Miami Dolphins

10. Lord's

# Game 22 Answers

**One-Minute Round**
1. Castleford Tigers; 2. 9 Innings in a Baseball Game; 3. Tennis; 4. Laura Kenny; 5. 1994; 6. 22; 7. Chile; 8. Wilfred LEGG, CHANCE Ruffin, Jack LAFFE

**Mystery Guest**
Michael Johnson, Andy Murray

**Home or Away**
1. Football. Jamie Vardy
2. Darts. Raymond van Barneveld

1. Tennis. Belgium
2. Horse Racing. Ruby Walsh

1. Rugby Union. Serge Blanco
2. Swimming. Mark Spitz

1. Cricket. Somerset
2. Sailing. America's Cup

**Top Ten**
Mike Hawthorn
Graham Hill
Jim Clark
John Surtees
Jackie Stewart
James Hunt
Nigel Mansell
Damon Hill
Lewis Hamilton
Jenson Button

**Buzzer Round**
1. Equestrian; 2. Eagles; 3. Chris Evert; 4. Edinburgh; 5. Peter Ebdon; 6. Edmonton; 7. Eusébio; 8. Ernie Els; 9. Épée; 10. Essex

# Game 23

# One-Minute Round

1.  Which Rugby Union team play their home games at Kingston Park?

2.  Can you solve this sporting equation? '6 CLT for L'

3.  In which sport do you have a Lead, a Second, a Third and a Skip?

4.  'HOT CANDLE' is an anagram of which athletics event?

5.  In which year did Paul Lawrie win the Open Championship?

6.  What is the minimum number of points needed to win a game of badminton?

7.  Camilo Villegas and James Rodríguez have both represented which country?

8.  These three sports stars all share parts of their names with jobs in the food industry...

    Brian **?** (Motor Sport)
    Terry **?** (Football)
    Chris **?** (Swimming)

# Mystery Guest

**In this round you are given three clues
to a sports star's identity.**

*Who is this Mystery Guest?*

1.  I made my English football league debut on loan at Preston North End in 1994.

2.  I hold the record for the most England caps earned while playing abroad.

3.  I own the MLS team Inter Miami FC.

*Who is this Mystery Guest?*

1.  I was born in 1969, and won four gold medals on the track for Team GB in Barcelona.

2.  I won the London Wheelchair Marathon six times between 1992 and 2002.

3.  I was named BBC Wales Sports Personality of the Year three times.

# Home or Away

**In this round there is a choice of a home question
for one point or an away question for two.**

*Do you want a home question on Rugby Union for one point or an
away question on the Winter Olympics for two?*

1.  **Rugby Union.** Who scored the first of his 58 tries for his country in
    2000 against Italy, and the last, 11 years later, against Australia?

2.  **Winter Olympics.** In which North American city did Amy
    Williams win Great Britain's only gold medal at the 2010
    Winter Olympics?

*Do you want a home question on Golf for one point or an away
question on Cycling for two?*

1.  **Golf.** Who was the only player to win all five of their matches at the
    2018 Ryder Cup at Le Golf National in France?

2.  **Cycling.** Who won Individual Pursuit Olympic gold for Great
    Britain in Barcelona, and two years later won a stage of the Tour de
    France for the first time?

*Do you want a home question on Athletics for one point or an away question on Netball for two?*

1. **Athletics.** In which Scandinavian city did triple jumper Jonathan Edwards win world championship gold in 1995, and in the process set a new world record?

2. **Netball.** Who played for her country at the 1998 Commonwealth Games in Kuala Lumpur and, 20 years later, coached them to their first ever Commonwealth title?

*Do you want a home question on Football for one point or an away question on Snooker for two?*

1. **Football.** Whose 21 goals for Spurs won him the Golden Boot in the first Premier League season?

2. **Snooker.** Which Snooker player lost to John Higgins in the 2011 World Championship final, but won the title against the same player eight year later?

# Top Ten

**As of the end of 2019, name the ten male cricketers to have made the most Test appearances for England.**

There's a point for each one you correctly identify, but guess one wrong and you lose your points from this round...

1 ......................................................................

2 ......................................................................

3 ......................................................................

4 ......................................................................

5 ......................................................................

6 ......................................................................

7 ......................................................................

8 ......................................................................

9 ......................................................................

10 ......................................................................

# Buzzer Round

**All the questions in this round are about the Netherlands and sports stars from that country...**

1. Which football team has won the most Eredivisie titles?

2. Dutchman Richard Krajicek won the Wimbledon Men's Singles title in which year?

3. In which sport have the Netherlands won the most Winter Olympic medals?

4. Which darts player is a five-time World Champion across the BDO and PDC competitions?

5. Over which distance has Dafne Schippers won two World Championship gold medals?

6. Which country did the Netherlands beat in a huge shock in the opening game of the 2009 T20 Cricket World Cup?

7. Daan Huizing and which other player represented Netherlands at the 2018 World Cup of Golf?

8. Max Verstappen started his Formula One career racing for which team?

9. Which Scandinavian country did the Netherlands beat in the final to win the Women's Euros in 2017?

10. In which sport are Sanne Wevers and Epke Zonderland both Olympic champions?

# Sprint Finish

**Describe these ten sporting words
and phrases to your team...**

1. Pat Cash

2. Season ticket

3. Putting green

4. New York Yankees

5. Jimmy White

6. Boxing promoter

7. Diving

8. Break point

9. The Derby

10. Leeds Rhinos

# Game 23 Answers

**One-Minute Round**
1. Newcastle Falcons; 2. 6 Champions League Titles for Liverpool; 3. Curling;
4. Decathlon; 5. 1999; 6. 21; 7. Colombia; 8. Brian BAKER, Terry BUTCHER,
Chris COOK

**Mystery Guest**
David Beckham, Tanni Grey-Thompson

**Home or Away**
1. Rugby Union. Shane Williams
2. Winter Olympics. Vancouver

1. Golf. Francesco Molinari
2. Cycling. Chris Boardman

1. Athletics. Gothenburg
2. Netball. Tracey Neville

1. Football. Teddy Sheringham
2. Snooker. Judd Trump

**Top Ten**
Alastair Cook
James Anderson
Stuart Broad
Alec Stewart
Ian Bell
Graham Gooch
David Gower
Michael Atherton
Colin Cowdrey
Geoffrey Boycott

**Buzzer Round**
1. Ajax; 2. 1996; 3. Speed Skating; 4. Raymond van Barneveld; 5. 200m;
6. England; 7. Joost Luiten; 8. Toro Rosso; 9. Denmark; 10. Gymnastics

# Game 24

# One-Minute Round

1. Which cricket team play their home games at Taunton?

2. Can you solve this sporting equation? '3GN for RR'

3. In which cycling race can you win the Coupe Omnisports?

4. 'EARL KEYRING' is an anagram of which England footballer?

5. In which year did Rugby League's Super League start?

6. How many reds are on the table at the start of a frame in snooker?

7. Félix Savón and Anier García have both won Olympic gold for which country?

8. These three sports stars all share their names with parts of the face…

   Tiffany **?** (Ice Skating)
   Seike **?** (Judo)
   Allen **?** (Baseball)

# Mystery Guest

**In this round you are given three clues
to a sports star's identity.**

*Who is this Mystery Guest?*

1. I was born in Sheffield in 1986.

2. In 2006, I won my first major medal, a bronze at the
   Commonwealth Games.

3. I won gold for Team GB at the 2012 Olympic Games, on
   'Super Saturday'.

*Who is this Mystery Guest?*

1. I burst onto the international scene by scoring four goals at
   Euro 2004.

2. In 2014, I became the seventh Manchester United captain in the
   Premier League era.

3. As of 2020, I am the record goal scorer for my country.

# Home or Away

**In this round there is a choice of a home question
for one point or an away question for two.**

*Do you want a home question on Tennis for one point or an away
question on Formula One for two?*

1.  **Tennis.** Which Czech tennis player won her first two Grand Slam
    singles finals, both at Wimbledon, before losing her third in 2019?

2.  **Formula One.** Niki Lauda, Alain Prost and Mika Häkkinen
    have all won F1 Drivers' World Championships whilst racing with
    which team?

*Do you want a home question on Rugby Union for one point or an
away question on the Olympics for two?*

1.  **Rugby Union.** In which year did New Zealand's David Kirk
    become the first captain to lift the Rugby Union World Cup?

2.  **The Olympics.** By winning Individual jumping gold in Rio at
    the age of 58, who became Britain's oldest Olympic gold medallist
    since 1908?

*Do you want a home question on Football for one point or an away question on Snooker for two?*

1. **Football.** Since 2010, which English club have won the Europa League, the Champions League and the Premier League?

2. **Snooker.** In 2018, who won his third World Snooker Championship, 15 years after winning his second?

*Do you want a home question on Cricket for one point or an away question on Baseball for two?*

1. **Cricket.** Which player scored over 5,000 runs and took over 100 wickets for England in his 197 One Day International matches?

2. **Baseball.** Which Major League Baseball team has the longest name in terms of letters?

# Top Ten

**Between 1975 and 2019, name the ten golfers to win the US Masters on more than one occasion.**

There's a point for each one you correctly identify, but guess one wrong and you lose your points from this round…

1 .................................................................

2 .................................................................

3 .................................................................

4 .................................................................

5 .................................................................

6 .................................................................

7 .................................................................

8 .................................................................

9 .................................................................

10 .................................................................

# Buzzer Round

**All the questions in this round are
about the 1996 Summer Olympics...**

1.  In 1996, who became the first man to win both the 200m and 400m
    at the same games?

2.  Which sporting icon lit the stadium cauldron during the opening
    ceremony?

3.  Beach Volleyball featured for the first time as an official sport at the
    Olympics; which South American country won gold and silver in the
    women's competition?

4.  In which sport did Cuba top the medal table with seven medals,
    including four golds?

5.  Which American won the women's tennis singles gold medal, three
    years before winning Wimbledon?

6.  In which sport did Great Britain win their only gold medal of
    the games?

7.  Footballers Celestine Babayaro, Daniel Amokachi and Emmanuel
    Amunike scored the goals for which country as they won the gold
    medal match?

8.  Which five-time Tour de France winner won gold in the Time Trial
    for Spain?

9. Gold medals were awarded in Mistral, Tornado, Laser and Soling events in which sport?

10. Which heptathlete was the only woman to win an athletics medal for Great Britain at the games?

# Sprint Finish

**Describe these ten sporting words
and phrases to your team...**

1. FA Cup Final

2. Last leg

3. Swimming costume

4. Golden duck

5. Water polo

6. Kelly Holmes

7. Penalty try

8. Caddy

9. Nottingham Forest

10. Smash

# Game 24 Answers

**One-Minute Round**

1. Somerset; 2. 3 Grand Nationals for Red Rum; 3. Tour de France; 4. Gary Lineker; 5. 1996; 6. 15; 7. Cuba; 8. Tiffany CHIN, Seike NOSE, Allen GUM

**Mystery Guest**

Jessica Ennis-Hill, Wayne Rooney

**Home or Away**

1. Tennis. Petra Kvitová
2. Formula One. McLaren

1. Rugby Union. 1987
2. The Olympics. Nick Skelton

1. Football. Chelsea
2. Snooker. Mark Williams

1. Cricket. Paul Collingwood
2. Baseball. Philadelphia Phillies

**Top Ten**

Tom Watson
Seve Ballesteros
Jack Nicklaus
Nick Faldo
Bernhard Langer
Ben Crenshaw
José María Olazábal
Tiger Woods
Phil Mickelson
Bubba Watson

**Buzzer Round**

1. Michael Johnson; 2. Muhammad Ali; 3. Brazil; 4. Boxing; 5. Lindsay Davenport; 6. Rowing; 7. Nigeria; 8. Miguel Induráin; 9. Sailing; 10. Denise Lewis

# Game 25

# One-Minute Round

1. Which English football team play their home games at Prenton Park?

2. Can you solve this sporting equation? '3 OC for SB'

3. In which sport can you win the Bledisloe Cup?

4. 'OILMAN WHISTLE' is an anagram of which World Champion?

5. In which year did Rebecca Adlington win two Olympic gold medals?

6. How many players are there in a field hockey team?

7. Suzann Pettersen and Joshua King have both represented which country?

8. These three sports stars all share parts of their names with types of money...

   Raheem **?** (Football)
   **?** Smolej (Skiing)
   Cameron **?** (Basketball)

# Mystery Guest

**In this round you are given three clues
to a sports star's identity.**

### Who is this Mystery Guest?

1.  I was born in São Paulo in 1960.

2.  I am a three-time Formula One champion.

3.  I tragically lost my life in an accident at the 1994 San Marino
    Grand Prix.

### Who is this Mystery Guest?

1.  I had the most successful period of my career at Wigan Warriors,
    where I played between 1992 and 1996.

2.  I scored 26 tries for Great Britain over a six-year period.

3.  My nickname was 'Chariots'.

# Home or Away

In this round there is a choice of a home question
for one point or an away question for two.

*Do you want a home question on Rugby Union for one point or an
away question on Swimming for two?*

1. **Rugby Union.** On the 2017 Lions tour of New Zealand, which
   Irishman was captain in the first test but did not play in the second
   or third?

2. **Swimming.** Which Englishman, who specialised in the 50m
   Butterfly and 50m Freestyle, won six Short Course swimming world
   titles between 1993 and 2004?

*Do you want a home question on Golf for one point or an away
question on American Football for two?*

1. **Golf.** Which South African won the first of his majors in 1959 and
   his ninth and final one in 1978?

2. **American Football.** Which city have the Oakland Raiders
   relocated to from the start of the 2020 NFL season?

*Do you want a home question on Football for one point or an away question on Gymnastics for two?*

1. **Football.** Which club beat Real Madrid and Juventus in the knockout stages of the 2018–19 Champions League, before losing to English opposition in the semi-finals?

2. **Gymnastics.** Which gymnast won three gold medals at the 1972 Olympics and in 1988, was the first to be inducted into the International Gymnastics Hall of Fame?

*Do you want a home question on Athletics for one point or an away question on Rugby League for two?*

1. **Athletics.** Between 1997 and 2001, which American sprinter won three consecutive 100m World titles?

2. **Rugby League.** In 2018, who became the first non-British team to win the Challenge Cup in the competition's 117-year history?

# Top Ten

**Name the last ten host venues
of the Winter Olympics.**

There's a point for each one you correctly identify, but guess one
wrong and you lose your points from this round...

1 .............................................................

2 .............................................................

3 .............................................................

4 .............................................................

5 .............................................................

6 .............................................................

7 .............................................................

8 .............................................................

9 .............................................................

10 .............................................................

# Buzzer Round

**All the questions in this round are
about people whose surnames are Smith...**

1. Ben Smith, Conrad Smith and Aaron Smith all started for
   New Zealand in the 2015 Rugby Union World Cup Final against
   which team?

2. Footballer Kelly Smith had three different spells with which
   English team?

3. Michael Smith lost to which Dutch darts player in the 2019 PDC
   World Championship Final?

4. In which year did Leon Smith captain Great Britain to Davis Cup
   victory?

5. Tony Smith coached which Super League team to Grand Final wins
   in 2004 and 2007?

6. Athletics star Steve Smith won Olympic bronze for Great Britain in
   which field event in 1996?

7. In 2019, Australian Cameron Smith competed against the USA in
   which international golf tournament?

8. American Football running back Emmitt Smith won three Super
   Bowls in the 1990s with which team?

9. In 2005 at Taunton, for which county did Graeme Smith score his maiden first-class triple hundred?

10. In which city did English weightlifter Zoe Smith win Commonwealth gold in 2014?

# Sprint Finish

**Describe these ten sporting words
and phrases to your team...**

1. Usain Bolt

2. All-rounder

3. Grand slam

4. Bunker

5. Twickenham

6. Ian Thorpe

7. BMX

8. Gum shield

9. Drop ball

10. Sin bin

# Game 25 Answers

**One-Minute Round**

1. Tranmere Rovers; 2. 3 Open Championships for Seve Ballesteros; 3. Rugby Union; 4. Lewis Hamilton; 5. 2008; 6. 11; 7. Norway; 8. Raheem STERLING, FRANC Smolej, Cameron DOLLAR

**Mystery Guest**

Ayrton Senna, Martin Offiah

**Home or Away**

1. Rugby Union. Peter O'Mahony
2. Swimming. Mark Foster

1. Golf. Gary Player
2. American Football. Las Vegas

1. Football. Ajax
2. Gymnastics. Olga Korbut

1. Athletics. Maurice Greene
2. Rugby League. Catalans Dragons

**Top Ten**

PyeongChang
Sochi
Vancouver
Turin
Salt Lake City
Nagano
Lillehammer
Albertville
Calgary
Sarajevo

**Buzzer Round**

1. Australia; 2. Arsenal; 3. Michael van Gerwen; 4. 2015; 5. Leeds Rhinos; 6. High jump; 7. Presidents Cup; 8. Dallas Cowboys; 9. Somerset; 10. Glasgow

# Game 26

# One-Minute Round

1. What is the franchise name of the Major League Baseball team based in Arizona?

2. Can you solve this sporting equation? '300 = PS in TPB'

3. In which sport would you find the positions Libero and Setters?

4. 'UNMARRY DAY' is an anagram of which tennis star?

5. In which year did Celtic win football's European Cup?

6. How many laps are there in the Indianapolis 500?

7. Lorena Ochoa and Canelo Álvarez are both sports stars from which country?

8. These three sports stars all share parts of their names with things you might find in the barbers...

   Dino **?** (Basketball)
   **?** Shines (Baseball)
   Delphine **?** (Athletics)

# Mystery Guest

**In this round you are given three clues
to a sports star's identity.**

### Who is this Mystery Guest?

1. I made my Test debut at the age of 16 in 1989.

2. In 2010, I became the first player to score a double-century in ODI cricket.

3. I have scored 100 centuries in international cricket for India.

### Who is this Mystery Guest?

1. I have won over 160 international caps for my country.

2. I was a World Cup-winning captain at the 2019 Women's World Cup.

3. I won the Ballon d'Or in 2019.

# Home or Away

**In this round there is a choice of a home question for one point or an away question for two.**

*Do you want a home question on Football for one point or an away question on Horse Racing for two?*

1.  **Football.** In 2011, which Manchester United player became the first overseas player to score five goals in a Premier League game?

2.  **Horse Racing.** Which Champion Jockey won the 2018 Cheltenham Gold Cup on Native River, 18 years after winning the race for the first time on Looks Like Trouble?

*Do you want a home question on Golf for one point or an away question on Formula One for two?*

1.  **Golf.** Which American's two major wins, the Open Championship and the US Masters, both came in 1998?

2.  **Formula One.** Who finished in the top three of the Formula One Drivers' Championship for three consecutive years between 1993 and 1995, before winning his only World Title the year after?

*Do you want a home question on Cricket for one point or an away question on Cycling for two?*

1. **Cricket.** England, Australia and which other country are the only teams to have won the Women's Cricket World Cup?

2. **Cycling.** In 2018, which British cyclist became the first rider to hold all three Grand Tour winners' jerseys at the same time in 25 years?

*Do you want a home question on Tennis for one point or an away question on the Winter Olympics for two?*

1. **Tennis.** Who won the 2003 French Open, his only Grand Slam, and in the same year became only the second Spanish man to top the world rankings?

2. **Winter Olympics.** In which event did Izzy Atkin win Great Britain's first Winter Olympic medal on skis?

# Top Ten

**Name the ten people that have won
World Athletics Championship individual
gold for Great Britain since 2000.**

There's a point for each one you correctly identify, but guess one
wrong and you lose your points from this round…

1 ................................................................

2 ................................................................

3 ................................................................

4 ................................................................

5 ................................................................

6 ................................................................

7 ................................................................

8 ................................................................

9 ................................................................

10 ................................................................

# Buzzer Round

**All the questions in this round are about coaches and managers...**

1. Which Wimbledon Ladies' Singles Champion coached Andy Murray between 2014 and 2016?

2. In 2019, Toto Wolff led which Formula One team to a sixth consecutive Constructors' Championship?

3. Rob McCracken is a leading British coach in which sport?

4. Which football manager led Blackburn Rovers to the Premier League title in 1995?

5. Which Rugby Union coach led the British and Irish Lions to a series win in 2013 against Australia?

6. Steve Kerr coached which basketball team to three NBA Championship titles between 2015 and 2018?

7. In which sport has World Champion Terry Griffiths coached Barry Hawkins, Ali Carter and Marco Fu?

8. Brian Noble led which Rugby League team to the Super League title in 2001, 2003 and 2005?

9. Mel Marshall coached which British swimmer to Olympic gold in Rio?

10. Which former South African batsman led India to Cricket World Cup victory in 2011?

# Sprint Finish

**Describe these ten sporting words
and phrases to your team...**

1. Slalom

2. Nightwatchman

3. Olympic torch

4. Aston Villa

5. Will Carling

6. Putter

7. Fencing

8. Check out

9. Scoreboard

10. AP McCoy

# **Game 26** Answers

## One-Minute Round
1. Diamondbacks; 2. 300 = Perfect Score in Ten Pin Bowling; 3. Volleyball;
4. Andy Murray; 5. 1967; 6. 200; 7. Mexico; 8. Dino HAIR, RAZOR Shines,
Delphine COMBE

## Mystery Guest
Sachin Tendulkar, Megan Rapinoe

## Home or Away
1.  Football. Dimitar Berbatov
2.  Horse Racing. Richard Johnson

1.  Golf. Mark O'Meara
2.  Formula One. Damon Hill

1.  Cricket. New Zealand
2.  Cycling. Chris Froome

1.  Tennis. Juan Carlos Ferrero
2.  Winter Olympics. Freestyle Skiing

## Top Ten
Dina Asher-Smith
Katarina Johnson-Thompson
Mo Farah
Jessica Ennis-Hill
Greg Rutherford
Christine Ohuruogu
Dai Greene
Phillips Idowu
Paula Radcliffe
Jonathan Edwards

## Buzzer Round
1. Amelie Maurésmo; 2. Mercedes; 3. Boxing; 4. Kenny Dalglish; 5. Warren
Gatland; 6. Golden State Warriors; 7. Snooker; 8. Bradford Bulls; 9. Adam Peaty;
10. Gary Kirsten

# Game 27

# One-Minute Round

1. Which American football team play their home games in the NFL at Mile High?

2. Can you solve this sporting equation? '7FOWT for MS'

3. In which sport are events competed at 3m and 10m at the Olympics?

4. 'IMPORTANT ANN HOSTS' is an anagram of which Rugby Union team?

5. In which year did Bob Willis take 8 for 43 against Australia at Headingley?

6. How many players are there on an Aussie Rules team?

7. Barbara Strýcová and Jan Železný have both represented which country?

8. These three sports stars all share parts of their names with Presidents of the USA…

   MaliVai **?** (Tennis)
   **?** Woods (Boxing)
   Judd **?** (Snooker)

# Mystery Guest

**In this round you are given three clues to a sports star's identity.**

*Who is this Mystery Guest?*

1. I was the Lancashire schools under-11 chess champion.

2. I took a hat-trick in my last ODI for England.

3. I was named 'Man of the Series' in the 2005 Ashes.

*Who is this Mystery Guest?*

1. I'm an American swimmer born in 1950.

2. I was known for my famous moustache.

3. I won seven gold medals at the 1972 Munich Olympics, and have nine in total.

# Home or Away

**In this round there is a choice of a home question
for one point or an away question for two.**

*Do you want a home question on Football for one point or an
away question on Snooker for two?*

1.  **Football.** Which country did England play twice at the 2018 FIFA
    World Cup, losing to them on both occasions?

2.  **Snooker.** In 2005, who, at the age of 22, became only the third
    person to win the World Snooker Championship as a qualifier?

*Do you want a home question on Athletics for one point or an
away question on the Winter Olympics for two?*

1.  **Athletics.** In 1990, which British star set a World Record of 90.98m
    as well as winning gold at the Commonwealth Games and European
    Championships?

2.  **Winter Olympics.** In which sport have Robin Cousins and John
    Curry both won Winter Olympic gold medals for Great Britain?

*Do you want a home question on Cricket for one point or an away question on Horse Racing for two?*

1. **Cricket.** In 2010, which New Zealander became the first batsman to score 1,000 runs in international T20 cricket?

2. **Horse Racing.** Which famous horse did Lester Piggott ride to victory when it completed English flat racing's Triple Crown in 1970?

*Do you want a home question on Tennis for one point or an away question on Formula One for two?*

1. **Tennis.** What is the name of the tournament that Switzerland's Belinda Bencic and Roger Federer won together in 2018 and 2019?

2. **Formula One.** Which double World Champion is the only driver from his country to win a Formula One Grand Prix?

# Top Ten

**Name the ten players that have scored the most
Premier League goals as of the start of 2020.**

There's a point for each one you correctly identify, but guess one
wrong and you lose your points from this round...

1  ................................................................

2  ................................................................

3  ................................................................

4  ................................................................

5  ................................................................

6  ................................................................

7  ................................................................

8  ................................................................

9  ................................................................

10  ................................................................

# Buzzer Round

**All the questions in this round are about France
and sports stars from that country...**

1. After racing around Paris on the final stage of the Tour de France, on which famous street do cyclists cross the finish line?

2. Which French Formula One driver won four World Championships between 1985 and 1993?

3. In which year did Marion Bartoli win the Wimbledon Ladies' Singles title?

4. In 2015, Toulon beat which fellow French team in the final of the European Champions Cup?

5. Who was the winning captain of the 2018 Ryder Cup, the first to be held in France?

6. Eunice Barber is a World Champion in Heptathlon and which other event?

7. What are the current Rugby League team called that play in Super League but are based in France?

8. Which country did France beat in the final as they won the FIFA World Cup in 1998?

9. Frenchman Tony Parker won four NBA titles whilst playing for which team?

10. In which motor sport is Sébastien Loeb a nine-time World Champion?

# Sprint Finish

**Describe these ten sporting words
and phrases to your team...**

1. On the ropes

2. Queen's Club

3. Phil Taylor

4. Photo finish

5. Super League

6. Chelsea

7. Third umpire

8. Synchronised swimming

9. The haka

10. Winger

# Game 27 Answers

**One-Minute Round**
1. Denver Broncos; 2. 7 Formula One World Titles for Michael Schumacher;
3. Diving; 4. Northampton Saints; 5. 1981; 6. 18; 7. Czech Republic; 8. MaliVai
WASHINGTON, CLINTON Woods, Judd TRUMP

**Mystery Guest**
Andrew Flintoff, Mark Spitz

**Home or Away**
1. Football. Belgium
2. Snooker. Shaun Murphy

1. Athletics. Steve Backley
2. Winter Olympics. Figure Skating

1. Cricket. Brendon McCullum
2. Horse Racing. Nijinsky

1. Tennis. Hopman Cup
2. Formula One. Fernando Alonso

**Top Ten**
Alan Shearer
Wayne Rooney
Andrew Cole
Frank Lampard
Sergio Agüero
Thierry Henry
Robbie Fowler
Jermain Defoe
Michael Owen
Les Ferdinand

**Buzzer Round**
1. Champs-Élysées; 2. Alain Prost; 3. 2013; 4. ASM Clermont Auvergne;
5. Thomas Bjørn; 6. Long jump; 7. Catalans Dragons; 8. Brazil; 9. San Antonio
Spurs; 10. Rallying

# Game 28

# One-Minute Round

1. In which city is snooker's UK Championship held at the Barbican Centre?

2. Can you solve this sporting equation? '16WC for PT'

3. In which sport does a domestique help the other members of the team?

4. 'PERSONATING WETLANDS' is an anagram of which American Football team?

5. In which year did Darren Clarke win the Open Championship?

6. Over what distance is the longest Olympic swimming event in the pool in metres?

7. Jumbo Ozaki and Takuma Sato have both represented which country?

8. These three sports stars all share parts of their names with places you might find fish...

   ? Williams (American Football)
   Lennie ? (Motor Racing)
   ? Gaw (Baseball)

# Mystery Guest

**In this round you are given three clues
to a sports star's identity.**

### Who is this Mystery Guest?

1. I won my only Olympic silver at my first games in 2000.

2. I competed in the Le Mans 24-hour endurance race for the first time in 2016.

3. I won six gold medals in cycling, winning the last of them at the 2012 Olympics.

### Who is this Mystery Guest?

1. I was nicknamed the Sparrow from Minsk.

2. I retired from gymnastics in 1977, at the age of 22.

3. I won two silver and four gold medals at the 1972 and 1976 Olympic Games in gymnastics.

# Home or Away

**In this round there is a choice of a home question
for one point or an away question for two.**

*Do you want a home question on Cricket for one point or an away
question on Rowing for two?*

1.  **Cricket.** Which Australian became the first player to hit 100 sixes in
    Test cricket?

2.  **Rowing.** After winning three consecutive Olympic rowing silver
    medals, who won her first gold in London in the Double Sculls?

*Do you want a home question on Football for one point or an
away question on Boxing for two?*

1.  **Football.** Barnsley, Blackpool and which other team are the only
    clubs to have spent just one season in the Premier League?

2.  **Boxing.** Who became the first boxer to win a World Title at eight
    different weight divisions?

*Do you want a home question on Golf for one point or an away question on Formula One for two?*

1. **Golf.** Between 1990 and 2020, who was the only Scottish golfer to win a major?

2. **Formula One.** Who was the only Englishman to win a Formula One World title between 1975 and 1990?

*Do you want a home question on Rugby Union for one point or an away question on the Winter Olympics for two?*

1. **Rugby Union.** At which stadium did Wales play their home games between 1997 and 1999?

2. **Winter Olympics.** The USA has hosted the Winter Olympics on four different occasions, but which venue has hosted the games twice?

# Top Ten

**In tennis, name the ten countries that have
won the Davis Cup on the most occasions.**

There's a point for each one you correctly identify, but guess one
wrong and you lose your points from this round…

1 ...........................................................................

2 ...........................................................................

3 ...........................................................................

4 ...........................................................................

5 ...........................................................................

6 ...........................................................................

7 ...........................................................................

8 ...........................................................................

9 ...........................................................................

10 ...........................................................................

# Buzzer Round

**The answers to all the questions in this round begin
with the letter M. In the case of a person, it's the
surname that will begin with that letter...**

1. Which football team play their home games at The Den?

2. Which Scottish golfer captained Europe at the 2010 Ryder Cup?

3. Which Irish rugby union team play their home games at
   Thomond Park?

4. Which West Indian fast bowler took 376 Test wickets between 1978
   and 1991?

5. Which tennis player won the Women's Singles French Open in 2016
   and then Wimbledon the following year?

6. Which American state is home to major sports teams the Vikings
   and the Timberwolves?

7. Which driver won the 1992 Formula One World Championship?

8. The Carlton Blues, Collingwood Magpies and Hawthorn Hawks all
   play Aussie Rules in which city?

9. Which American was joint top goal scorer in the 2019 Women's
   World Cup?

10. Who won bronze for Great Britain as skip in the curling team at the
    2014 Winter Olympics?

# Sprint Finish

**Describe these ten sporting words
and phrases to your team...**

1. The Ashes

2. Diving board

3. Transfer window

4. Lawn bowls

5. Dan Carter

6. Chip shot

7. Ferrari

8. Butterfly

9. Lacrosse

10. Somersault

# Game 28 Answers

**One-Minute Round**
1. York; 2. 16 World Championships for Phil Taylor; 3. Cycling; 4. New England Patriots; 5. 2011; 6. 1500; 7. Japan; 8. TANK Williams, Lennie POND, CHIPPY Gaw

**Mystery Guest**
Chris Hoy, Olga Korbut

**Home or Away**
1. Cricket. Adam Gilchrist
2. Rowing. Katherine Grainger

1. Football. Swindon Town
2. Boxing. Manny Pacquiao

1. Golf. Paul Lawrie
2. Formula One. James Hunt

1. Rugby Union. Wembley
2. Winter Olympics. Lake Placid

**Top Ten**
USA
Australia
France
Great Britain
Sweden
Spain
Czech Republic
Germany
Croatia
Russia

**Buzzer Round**
1. Millwall; 2. Colin Montgomerie; 3. Munster; 4. Malcolm Marshall; 5. Garbiñe Muguruza; 6. Minnesota; 7. Nigel Mansell; 8. Melbourne; 9. Alex Morgan; 10. Eve Muirhead

# Game 29

# One-Minute Round

1. What is the franchise name of the Major League Baseball team based in Miami?

2. Can you solve this sporting equation? '169G at the 2018 WC'

3. In which sport does the term rope-a-dope originate?

4. 'THWACK MINE' is an anagram of which Rugby Union stadium?

5. In which year did Mike Powell break the long jump world record?

6. At the Commonwealth Games, what is the minimum number of points needed to win a game of squash?

7. Ken Doherty and Shane Lowry have both represented which country?

8. These three sports stars all share parts of their names with types of bread...

   Dennis ? (American Football)
   Sylvia ? (Volleyball)
   Bertrand ? (Motor Racing)

# Mystery Guest

**In this round you are given three clues
to a sports star's identity.**

### Who is this Mystery Guest?

1. I won my first major in 1989.

2. I handed Tiger Woods his first Green Jacket at the US Masters.

3. I won 25 points at the Ryder Cup and captained Europe in 2008.

### Who is this Mystery Guest?

1. My Formula One debut was for BMW Sauber at the 2007 US Grand Prix.

2. I hold the record for being the youngest ever World Champion as of 2019.

3. My four World Championships all came with Red Bull.

# Home or Away

In this round there is a choice of a home question
for one point or an away question for two.

*Do you want a home question on Cricket for one point or an away
question on Gymnastics for two?*

1.  **Cricket.** In 2011, which county won the County Championship title
    outright for the first time in 77 years?

2.  **Gymnastics.** Great Britain's Max Whitlock won Olympic bronze
    in 2012 and gold in 2016 in which event?

*Do you want a home question on Tennis for one point or an away
question on Motor Sport for two?*

1.  **Tennis.** Between 1989 and 2002, which Spaniard won 14 of the 31
    Grand Slam singles and doubles Finals in her career?

2.  **Motor Sport.** Between 2003 and 2018, Frenchmen Sébastien Ogier
    and Sébastien Loeb shared all 15 World titles in which sport?

*Do you want a home question on Football for one point or an
away question on Rugby League for two?*

1.  **Football.** Which goalkeeper has played 75 times for England and
    won two Premier League titles in a 12-year spell with one club?

2.  **Rugby League.** Which Premier League football ground hosts
    Super League's Grand Final every year?

*Do you want a home question on Golf for one point or an away
question on Ice Hockey for two?*

1.  **Golf.** Who was the first American golfer to become world number
    one, doing so in March 1992?

2.  **Ice Hockey.** Which NHL Ice Hockey team's franchise name comes
    last alphabetically?

# Top Ten

**In horse racing, name the ten British racecourses
that start with the letters C, D or E?**

There's a point for each one you correctly identify, but guess one
wrong and you lose your points from this round…

1 ................................................................

2 ................................................................

3 ................................................................

4 ................................................................

5 ................................................................

6 ................................................................

7 ................................................................

8 ................................................................

9 ................................................................

10 ................................................................

# Buzzer Round

**All the questions in this round are
about people called Sam...**

1. Sam Quek won Olympic hockey gold for Great Britain in 2016; which country did they beat in the final?

2. Sam Twiston-Davies is a leading competitor in which sport?

3. Which club did Sam Allardyce manage for more than 350 games between 1999 and 2007?

4. Which of the tennis majors did Australian Sam Stosur win in 2011?

5. Who captained the British and Irish Lions in 2013 and 2017?

6. Twin brothers Sam and Alex Lowes both compete in which form of racing?

7. In which year did Sam Torrance captain Europe to victory in the Ryder Cup?

8. Which British Rugby League player was awarded the Man of the Match medal in the 2014 Australian NRL Grand Final?

9. Which English cricketer made his Test debut against Pakistan in 2018 at Headingley?

10. Which Caribbean country is Baseball Hall of Fame player Sammy Sosa from?

# Sprint Finish

**Describe these ten sporting words
and phrases to your team...**

1. Rock climbing

2. Goal kick

3. Wicketkeeper

4. Tennis racket

5. José María Olazábal

6. Triathlon

7. Olympic rings

8. False start

9. Wheelie

10. Calcutta Cup

# Game 29 Answers

**One-Minute Round**

1. Marlins; 2. 169 Goals at the 2018 World Cup; 3. Boxing; 4. Twickenham;
5. 1991; 6. 11; 7. Ireland; 8. Dennis PITTA, Sylvia ROLL, Bertrand BAGUETTE

**Mystery Guest**

Nick Faldo, Sebastian Vettel

**Home or Away**

1. Cricket. Lancashire
2. Gymnastics. Pommel horse

1. Tennis. Arantxa Sánchez Vicario
2. Motor Sport. Rallying

1. Football. Joe Hart
2. Rugby League. Old Trafford

1. Golf. Fred Couples
2. Ice Hockey. Minnesota Wild

**Top Ten**

Carlisle
Cartmel
Catterick
Chelmsford City
Cheltenham
Chepstow
Chester
Doncaster
Epsom
Exeter

**Buzzer Round**

1. Netherlands; 2. Horse racing; 3. Bolton Wanderers; 4. US Open;
5. Sam Warburton; 6. Motorcycling; 7. 2002; 8. Sam Burgess; 9. Sam Curran;
10. Dominican Republic

# Game 30

# One-Minute Round

1. Which Rugby League team ground share with Sale Sharks?

2. Can you solve this sporting equation? '50M in an OSP'

3. Rugby's Giuseppe Garibaldi Trophy is contested between Italy and which other country?

4. 'CHAOS RINGER' is an anagram of which sport?

5. In which year did sailor Ellen MacArthur first set a world record for solo circumnavigation of the globe?

6. How many gymnastics events make up the Women's Individual All Around Olympic competition?

7. Katinka Hosszú and Zoltán Gera have both represented which country?

8. These three sports stars all share parts of their names with types of flooring...

   Vladimir **?** (Cycling)
   Devyn **?** (Basketball)
   Steve **?** (Football)

# Mystery Guest

**In this round you are given three clues
to a sports star's identity.**

## *Who is this Mystery Guest?*

1. I was born in 1973 in Yugoslavia.

2. I became the youngest woman to become tennis World
   Number One.

3. I won the last of my nine Grand Slam singles titles in 1996.

## *Who is this Mystery Guest?*

1. I was born in September 1956. I won four Olympic medals for
   Great Britain.

2. I was of one of 24 athletes inducted as inaugural members of the
   IAAF Hall of Fame.

3. In 1980, I simultaneously held world records in the mile, the 800,
   1000, and 1500 metres.

# Home or Away

**In this round there is a choice of a home question
for one point or an away question for two.**

*Do you want a home question on Tennis for one point or an away
question on Rowing for two?*

1. **Tennis.** By winning the US Open in 2019, Bianca Andreescu
   became the first Grand Slam Singles Champion from which country?

2. **Rowing.** Who won the last of his two Olympic medals in 2004, and
   then 15 years later won the Boat Race with Cambridge?

*Do you want a home question on Athletics for one point or an
away question on Ice Hockey for two?*

1. **Athletics.** Which British sprinter won 100m Olympic silver in
   2000 and, four years later, was part of the relay quartet that won
   gold in Athens?

2. **Ice Hockey.** What is the franchise name of the team that has most
   recently joined the NHL, based in Las Vegas?

*Do you want a home question on Football for one point or an away question on Snooker for two?*

1. **Football.** Which club lost to Everton in the 1984 FA Cup Final and in their next appearance in the final lost to Manchester City 6-0?

2. **Snooker.** In 2006, which Englishman became the Eight-Ball Pool World Champion and a year later lost in his first World Snooker Championship Final?

*Do you want a home question on Golf for one point or an away question on Formula One for two?*

1. **Golf.** Which five-time major champion golfer has finished second in the US Open on six occasions without ever winning it?

2. **Formula One.** Between 1970 and 1990, which was the only country to have three different F1 World Champions?

# Top Ten

**Name the last ten different winners of cricket's County Championship as of the start of 2020.**

There's a point for each one you correctly identify, but guess one wrong and you lose your points from this round...

1 ..................................................................

2 ..................................................................

3 ..................................................................

4 ..................................................................

5 ..................................................................

6 ..................................................................

7 ..................................................................

8 ..................................................................

9 ..................................................................

10 .................................................................

# Buzzer Round

**All the questions in this round are about South Africa
and sports stars from that country...**

1. Who captained South Africa to victory in the 2019 Rugby Union
   World Cup Final?

2. Over which distance did Caster Semenya win Olympic gold in both
   London and Rio?

3. Which South African tennis player lost to Novak Djokovic in the
   2018 Wimbledon Singles Final?

4. Who became the first from his country to score 13,000 runs in
   Test cricket?

5. In which sport did Jody Scheckter become World Champion in 1979?

6. Who became the first South African golfer to win all four majors?

7. In which year did South Africa become the first African country to
   host the FIFA World Cup?

8. In which sport have Natalie du Toit and Chad le Clos won
   Commonwealth gold medals?

9. In 2013, South African Daryl Impey wore the Yellow Jersey in which
   famous cycling race?

10. Which country defeated South Africa in the Netball World Cup
    Final in 1995?

# Sprint Finish

**Describe these ten sporting words
and phrases to your team...**

1. Set point

2. Fielder

3. Scrum

4. Amy Williams

5. Water hazard

6. Cover drive

7. Hammer throw

8. Pundit

9. Croquet

10. Shuttlecock

# Game 30 Answers

**One-Minute Round**

1. Salford Red Devils; 2. 50 Metres in an Olympic Swimming Pool; 3. France;
4. Horse racing; 5. 2005; 6. Four; 7. Hungary; 8. Vladimir KARPETS,
Devyn MARBLE, Steve STONE

**Mystery Guest**

Monica Seles, Sebastian Coe

**Home or Away**

1. Tennis. Canada
2. Rowing. James Cracknell

1. Athletics. Darren Campbell
2. Ice Hockey. Golden Knights

1. Football. Watford
2. Snooker. Mark Selby

1. Golf. Phil Mickelson
2. Formula One. Brazil

**Top Ten**

Essex
Surrey
Middlesex
Yorkshire
Durham
Warwickshire
Lancashire
Nottinghamshire
Sussex
Leicestershire

**Buzzer Round**

1. Siya Kolisi; 2. 800m; 3. Kevin Anderson; 4. Jacques Kallis; 5. Formula One;
6. Gary Player; 7. 2010; 8. Swimming; 9. Tour de France; 10. Australia

# Game 31

# One-Minute Round

1. What is the franchise name of the NHL Ice Hockey team based in Detroit?

2. Can you solve this sporting equation? '4P for a T in RL'

3. In which sport would you find the positions Centre and Wing Defence?

4. 'NAIL INDOOR ACTORS' is an anagram of which Ballon d'Or winner?

5. In which year did Denise Lewis win Olympic gold in the heptathlon?

6. In horse racing, how many English Classics are there?

7. Luca Brecel and Elise Mertens have both represented which country?

8. These three sports stars all share parts of their names with months of the year…

   **?** Sykes (Basketball)
   Solly **?** (Football)
   **?** Pikker (Wrestling)

# Mystery Guest

**In this round you are given three clues
to a sports star's identity.**

## *Who is this Mystery Guest?*

1.  I broke Thierry Henry's 21-year record as the youngest-ever first-team player for AS Monaco.

2.  In 2018, I became the second teenager, after Pelé, to score in a World Cup Final.

3.  I became the second most expensive footballer in history when I signed for Paris Saint-Germain.

## *Who is this Mystery Guest?*

1.  I was born in Stockholm on 6 June 1956.

2.  Although I was most famous for my performances on the court, I have also launched a successful range of underwear.

3.  I won five consecutive Wimbledon titles between 1976 and 1980.

# Home or Away

**In this round there is a choice of a home question for one point or an away question for two.**

*Do you want a home question on Rugby Union for one point or an away question on Darts for two?*

1. **Rugby Union.** Who won the World Cup in 2015 and was named IRB World Player of the Year back to back the two years after?

2. **Darts.** What is the lowest number you cannot score with one dart on a standard dartboard?

*Do you want a home question on Football for one point or an away question on the Olympics for two?*

1. **Football.** Which South American player scored 69 goals in the Premier League, including three hat-tricks against Norwich City?

2. **The Olympics.** Which American city has hosted the Summer Olympics on two occasions, first in 1932 and again in 1984?

*Do you want a home question on Golf for one point or an away question on Formula One for two?*

1. **Golf.** Which English course hosted the Ryder Cup in 1985, 1989 and 1993?

2. **Formula One.** In 1997, which Canadian became the first driver from his country to win the Formula One World Championship?

*Do you want a home question on Cricket for one point or an away question on Ice Hockey for two?*

1. **Cricket.** Which was the only country other than Australia to win the men's Cricket World Cup between 1999 and 2015?

2. **Ice Hockey.** Which Canadian team has won the Stanley Cup on the most occasions?

# Top Ten

**Name the ten female winners of BBC Sports Personality of the Year between 1969 and 2019.**

There's a point for each one you correctly identify, but guess one wrong and you lose your points from this round...

1 ...............................................................

2 ...............................................................

3 ...............................................................

4 ...............................................................

5 ...............................................................

6 ...............................................................

7 ...............................................................

8 ...............................................................

9 ...............................................................

10 ..............................................................

# Buzzer Round

The answers to all the questions in this round
begin with the letter W. In the case of a person it's
the surname that will begin with that letter...

1. Which Australian dismissed Mike Gatting with the 'Ball of the Century' in 1993?

2. In which sport would you perform a 'clean and jerk'?

3. Which Rugby League team won the Challenge Cup in 2019?

4. Which Danish tennis player won her only Grand Slam at the 2018 Australian Open?

5. In which American city are major sports teams the Wizards and the Capitals based?

6. Which Welsh golfer won the US Masters in 1991?

7. Which British woman won Taekwondo bronze at the Rio Olympics?

8. Which capital city hosted one of the semi-finals of the UEFA European Championships in 2012?

9. Richard Dunwoody rode which horse to victory in the 1986 Grand National at Aintree?

10. Which Australian Formula One driver won nine Grand Prix races in his career?

# Sprint Finish

**Describe these ten sporting words
and phrases to your team...**

1.  Boxing

2.  Goodison Park

3.  Cricket whites

4.  Time trial

5.  Sumo wrestling

6.  Flanker

7.  Safety shot

8.  World Championships

9.  Cathy Freeman

10. St Helens

# Game 31 Answers

**One-Minute Round**

1. Red Wings; 2. 4 Points for a Try in Rugby League; 3. Netball; 4. Cristiano Ronaldo; 5. 2000; 6. Five; 7. Belgium; 8. APRIL Sykes, Solly MARCH, AUGUST Pikker

**Mystery Guest**

Kylian Mbappé, Björn Borg

**Home or Away**

1. Rugby Union. Beauden Barrett
2. Darts. 23

1. Football. Luis Suárez
2. The Olympics. Los Angeles

1. Golf. The Belfry
2. Formula One. Jacques Villeneuve

1. Cricket. India
2. Ice Hockey. Montréal Canadiens

**Top Ten**

Ann Jones
Anne, Princess Royal
Mary Peters
Virginia Wade
Jayne Torvill
Fatima Whitbread
Liz McColgan
Paula Radcliffe
Kelly Holmes
Zara Phillips

**Buzzer Round**

1. Shane Warne; 2. Weightlifting; 3. Warrington Wolves; 4. Caroline Wozniacki; 5. Washington, D.C.; 6. Ian Woosnam; 7. Bianca Walkden; 8. Warsaw; 9. West Tip; 10. Mark Webber

# Game 32

# One-Minute Round

1. What is the franchise name of the Major League Baseball team based in Houston?

2. Can you solve this sporting equation? '170 = HC in D'

3. Which country's top-flight domestic rugby competition is called the Currie Cup?

4. 'KINDEST PAGES' is an anagram of which winter sport?

5. In which year did Alex Ferguson become manager of Manchester United?

6. How many players are there on a hurling team?

7. Yelena Isinbayeva and Alexander Popov have both represented which country at the Olympics?

8. These three sports stars all share parts of their names with fruit...

   Francis **?** (Baseball)
   Mark **?** (Speedway)
   Don **?** (Ice Hockey)

# Mystery Guest

**In this round you are given three clues
to a sports star's identity.**

### Who is this Mystery Guest?

1. I'm a gymnast who grew up in Texas.

2. In 2019, I won my 25th World Championship medal, surpassing the previous record.

3. I won four gold medals at the 2016 Olympic Games, all coming before my 20th birthday.

### Who is this Mystery Guest?

1. I won the Premier League on 11 occasions between 1995 and 2013.

2. I played as a midfielder, appearing 499 times in the Premier League for the same club.

3. I briefly managed Oldham Athletic.

# Home or Away

In this round there is a choice of a home question
for one point or an away question for two.

*Do you want a home question on Cricket for one point or an away
question on Rugby League for two?*

1. **Cricket.** Which Australian batsman scored four consecutive 50s in
   the 2019 Ashes, despite missing the first Test?

2. **Rugby League.** Which club have won the Super League Grand
   Final seven times and previously played their home games at
   Knowsley Road?

*Do you want a home question on Golf for one point or an away
question on the Winter Olympics for two?*

1. **Golf.** Which course has hosted the Open Championship on more
   occasions than any other, with the most recent winner there being
   Zach Johnson?

2. **Winter Olympics.** Sprinter Craig Pickering won a bronze medal at
   the 2007 World Athletics Championships, before changing sports to
   join the British squad in which winter event?

*Do you want a home question on Football for one point or an away question on Formula One for two?*

1.  **Football.** Which country won football's European Championship in 2016, and three years later won the inaugural Nations League?

2.  **Formula One.** Which Australian won the World Championship for the third and final time in 1966?

*Do you want a home question on Tennis for one point or an away question on American Football for two?*

1.  **Tennis.** Andy Murray has won three Grand Slam singles finals, two against Novak Djokovic; who did he beat in the other?

2.  **American Football.** Which NFL team's franchise name comes first alphabetically?

# Top Ten

**Name the ten Englishmen to reach a World Snooker Championship Final between 1980 and 2010?**

There's a point for each one you correctly identify, but guess one wrong and you lose your points from this round…

1 ................................................................

2 ................................................................

3 ................................................................

4 ................................................................

5 ................................................................

6 ................................................................

7 ................................................................

8 ................................................................

9 ................................................................

10 ...............................................................

# Buzzer Round

**All the questions in this round are about
the 2012 Summer Olympics in London...**

1. Which sport was held at Horse Guards Parade during the 2012 Olympics?

2. Which former England international defender coached the men's Great Britain football team at the Games?

3. Which country won their first Women's Gymnastic Artistic Team All-Around gold medal since 1996?

4. Who set an Olympic Record time of 9.63 seconds in the men's 100m final?

5. Which boxer won Ireland's only gold at the 2012 Olympics?

6. Which Grand Slam champion did Andy Murray beat in the gold medal match held on Centre Court at Wimbledon?

7. Chris Hoy won which individual event at London 2012 to win his sixth and final Olympic gold?

8. Which Asian country topped the medal table in Archery at the 2012 Games?

9. Where did all the rowing events take place during the Games?

10. In which sport did Kenya win all of their 13 medals at the London Olympics?

# Sprint Finish

**Describe these ten sporting words
and phrases to your team...**

1. Judo

2. Overhead kick

3. Pacemaker

4. Jockey

5. Leicester Tigers

6. Golf tee

7. Oar

8. Kelly Sotherton

9. Penalty box

10. Figure skating

# **Game 32** Answers

**One-Minute Round**
1. Astros; 2. 170 = Highest Checkout in Darts; 3. South Africa; 4. Speed skating;
5. 1986; 6. 15; 7. Russia; 8. Francis MANGO, Mark LEMON, Don CHERRY

**Mystery Guest**
Simone Biles, Paul Scholes

**Home or Away**
1. Cricket. Marnus Labuschagne
2. Rugby League. St Helens

1. Golf. St Andrews
2. Winter Olympics. Bobsleigh

1. Football. Portugal
2. Formula One. Jack Brabham

1. Tennis. Milos Raonic
2. American Football. Chicago Bears

**Top Ten**
Steve Davis
Jimmy White
Joe Johnson
John Parrott
Nigel Bond
Peter Ebdon
Ronnie O'Sullivan
Shaun Murphy
Mark Selby
Ali Carter

**Buzzer Round**
1. Beach volleyball; 2. Stuart Pearce; 3. USA; 4. Usain Bolt; 5. Katie Taylor;
6. Roger Federer; 7. Keirin; 8. South Korea; 9. Eton Dorney; 10. Athletics

# Game 33

# One-Minute Round

1. Which Super Bowl winners play their home games in the NFL at Arrowhead Stadium?

2. Can you solve this sporting equation? '53EG for WR'

3. In which sport are the terms pogie and catch a crab used?

4. 'YOUNG BRUIN' is an anagram of which sport?

5. In which year did Nico Rosberg win the Formula One World Championship?

6. How many players are there on a handball team?

7. Belinda Bencic and Sébastien Buemi have both represented which country?

8. These three sports stars all share parts of their names with words that can come after OLYMPIC...

   Bobby ? (Boxing)
   ? Delhi (Baseball)
   Gary ? (Football)

# Mystery Guest

**In this round you are given three clues
to a sports star's identity.**

## *Who is this Mystery Guest?*

1. I beat Mark Philippoussis in my first Grand Slam Final appearance.

2. I won the Davis Cup in 2014, alongside compatriot Stanislas Wawrinka.

3. I have won the Wimbledon Men's Singles title a record eight times.

## *Who is this Mystery Guest?*

1. I am nicknamed the Baltimore Bullet.

2. In 2008, I broke the record for the most golds won at a single Olympic Games.

3. I'm the most successful Olympian of all time, winning 23 gold medals.

# Home or Away

**In this round there is a choice of a home question
for one point or an away question for two.**

*Do you want a home question on Football for one point or an
away question on Boxing for two?*

1. **Football.** Who took over as Everton manager in 2017 to become the
   first person to manage seven different teams in the Premier League?

2. **Boxing.** Which 1992 Lightweight Olympic Champion founded
   Golden Boy Promotions?

*Do you want a home question on Cricket for one point or an away
question on Horse Racing for two?*

1. **Cricket.** Which team won the County Championship in 2019, and
   in the same season won their first ever T20 Blast?

2. **Horse Racing.** On which horse did Tony McCoy finally win the
   Grand National at Aintree?

*Do you want a home question on Tennis for one point or an away question on the Olympics for two?*

1. **Tennis.** By winning the 1999 French Open, which American became the first man to win singles titles at all four Grand Slams as well as at the Olympics?

2. **The Olympics.** In Rio, South Korean Inbee Park won the first women's Olympic gold medal for over 100 years in which sport?

*Do you want a home question on Athletics for one point or an away question on Snooker for two?*

1. **Athletics.** Which American athlete won a record 13th World Championship gold medal when she won the 4x400m relay in Doha?

2. **Snooker.** Who, in 1983, became the first player to score a 147 maximum break at the World Snooker Championship?

# Top Ten

**Name the ten countries to provide a
men's golf major winner in the 2010s.**

There's a point for each one you correctly identify, but guess one
wrong and you lose your points from this round…

1 ................................................................

2 ................................................................

3 ................................................................

4 ................................................................

5 ................................................................

6 ................................................................

7 ................................................................

8 ................................................................

9 ................................................................

10 ................................................................

# Buzzer Round

**All the questions in this round are about Scotland
and sports stars from that country...**

1. Which team, in 1985, were the last club apart from Celtic and
   Rangers to win Scottish football's top division?

2. In which team sport have Kyle Coetzer, Calum MacLeod and Gavin
   Hamilton all represented Scotland?

3. Which Scottish woman won 10,000m gold at the 1991 World
   Championships?

4. Les Wallace, Jocky Wilson and Gary Anderson have all been World
   Champions in which sport?

5. As of 2020, who is his country's all-time record points scorer in
   Rugby Union?

6. Which golf course hosted the Ryder Cup in 2014?

7. In 2016, Katie Archibald won Olympic cycling gold in which event?

8. In which year did Stephen Hendry win his last World Snooker
   Championship?

9. Who partnered Scotsman Jamie Murray as he won the Wimbledon
   Mixed Doubles title in 2017?

10. Eve Muirhead is a World Champion skipper in which winter sport?

# Sprint Finish

**Describe these ten sporting words
and phrases to your team...**

1. Stadium

2. Swimming cap

3. Downhill skiing

4. Italia 90

5. Touchline

6. Pommel horse

7. Steve Redgrave

8. Benfica

9. Tyre change

10. Floodlights

# **Game 33** Answers

**One-Minute Round**
1. Kansas City Chiefs; 2. 53 England Goals for Wayne Rooney; 3. Rowing;
4. Rugby Union; 5. 2016; 6. Seven; 7. Switzerland; 8. Bobby RINGS,
FLAME Delhi, Gary MEDEL

**Mystery Guest**
Roger Federer, Michael Phelps

**Home or Away**
1. Football. Sam Allardyce
2. Boxing. Oscar De La Hoya

1. Cricket. Essex
2. Horse Racing. Don't Push It

1. Tennis. Andre Agassi
2. The Olympics. Golf

1. Athletics. Allyson Felix
2. Snooker. Cliff Thorburn

**Top Ten**
USA
Northern Ireland
South Africa
Germany
Australia
England
Sweden
Spain
Italy
Ireland

**Buzzer Round**
1. Aberdeen; 2. Cricket; 3. Liz McColgan; 4. Darts; 5. Chris Paterson;
6. Gleneagles; 7. Team Pursuit; 8. 1999; 9. Martina Hingis; 10. Curling

# Game 34

# One-Minute Round

1. Which cricket team play their home games in the County Championship at New Road?

2. Can you solve this sporting equation? '10T in the 2020 NS'

3. The Sheffield Shield is the domestic first-class cricket competition in which country?

4. 'HAM DIVED BACK' is an anagram of which footballer?

5. In which year did London host the World Athletics Championships?

6. How many teams currently play in the NFL?

7. Ato Boldon and Dwight Yorke have both represented which country?

8. These three sports stars all share parts of their names with alcoholic drinks…

   Michael **?** (Cricket)
   Bobby **?** (Baseball)
   **?** Burton (Golf)

# Mystery Guest

**In this round you are given three clues
to a sports star's identity.**

### *Who is this Mystery Guest?*

1.  I became the youngest ever World Champion in my sport, winning the title in 2005.

2.  I have also won the 24-hour Le Mans endurance race.

3.  As of the end of 2019, I am the only Spaniard to win a Formula One Grand Prix.

### *Who is this Mystery Guest?*

1.  I was named BBC Sports Personality of the Year in 1993.

2.  I have won gold medals at every major outdoor athletics championship.

3.  In 1992, I won Olympic gold in a time of 9.96 seconds.

# Home or Away

**In this round there is a choice of a home question
for one point or an away question for two.**

*Do you want a home question on Football for one point or an
away question on Basketball for two?*

1.  **Football.** Which French forward won the FIFA World Cup and
    Europa League in 2018, and a year later moved between two
    Spanish clubs for a fee of than more £100m?

2.  **Basketball.** Which NBA basketball team's franchise name comes
    last alphabetically?

*Do you want a home question on Rugby Union for one point or an
away question on Formula One for two?*

1.  **Rugby Union.** Which team won the first men's Rugby Sevens gold
    medal at the 2016 Rio Olympics?

2.  **Formula One.** Who won his fourth World title in 1993 and is the
    only man from his country to win the F1 World Championship?

*Do you want a home question on Golf for one point or an away question on Darts for two?*

1. **Golf.** In 2018, which golfer overtook Nick Faldo as the all-time leading points scorer for Europe in the Ryder Cup?

2. **Darts.** In 2008, the PDC World Darts Championship moved from the Circus Tavern to which North London venue?

*Do you want a home question on Cricket for one point or an away question on the Olympics for two?*

1. **Cricket.** In 2019, who became only the seventh Australian to score a Test triple century?

2. **The Olympics.** In which sport has Ian Millar competed at a record ten different Olympic Games?

# Top Ten

**Name the ten teams that have won the
most Premier League matches as of the
end of the 2019–20 football season.**

There's a point for each one you correctly identify, but guess one
wrong and you lose your points from this round...

1 ................................................................

2 ................................................................

3 ................................................................

4 ................................................................

5 ................................................................

6 ................................................................

7 ................................................................

8 ................................................................

9 ................................................................

10 ................................................................

# Buzzer Round

**All the questions in this round are about people
whose surnames are Jones...**

1. Who was England's wicketkeeper during the 2005 Ashes?

2. With which team did Vinnie Jones win the FA Cup in 1988?

3. In which sport did Jade Jones win Olympic gold in 2012 and 2016?

4. British snowboarder Jenny Jones won Winter Olympic bronze in 2014, in which city?

5. Who captained Wales to the Grand Slam in the 2008 Six Nations?

6. Leisel Jones is a three-time Olympic swimming champion from which country?

7. Which Welshman defeated boxer Roy Jones Jr to finish his career 46 fights undefeated?

8. In which decade did Britain's Ann Jones win the Wimbledon Ladies' Singles title?

9. With which Atlanta-based team has Julio Jones scored over 50 touchdowns in the NFL?

10. Which English constructor did Alan Jones drive for as he won the 1980 Formula One World Championship?

# Sprint Finish

**Describe these ten sporting words
and phrases to your team...**

1. Captain

2. Wimbledon

3. Cross-country skiing

4. Daley Thompson

5. Rhythmic gymnastics

6. Theatre of Dreams

7. Golf ball

8. Finish line

9. Third man

10. Touchdown

# Game 34 Answers

**One-Minute Round**
1. Worcestershire; 2. 10 Teams in the 2020 Netball Superleague; 3. Australia; 4. David Beckham; 5. 2017; 6. 32; 7. Trinidad and Tobago; 8. Michael BEER, Bobby WINE, BRANDIE Burton

**Mystery Guest**
Fernando Alonso, Linford Christie

**Home or Away**
1. Football. Antoine Griezmann
2. Basketball. Washington Wizards

1. Rugby Union. Fiji
2. Formula One. Alain Prost

1. Golf. Sergio García
2. Darts. Alexandra Palace

1. Cricket. David Warner
2. The Olympics. Equestrian

**Top Ten**
Manchester United
Arsenal
Chelsea
Liverpool
Tottenham Hotspur
Manchester City
Everton
Newcastle United
Aston Villa
West Ham United

**Buzzer Round**
1. Geraint Jones; 2. Wimbledon; 3. Taekwondo; 4. Sochi; 5. Ryan Jones; 6. Australia; 7. Joe Calzaghe; 8. 1960s; 9. Atlanta Falcons; 10. Williams

# Game 35

# One-Minute Round

1. What is the franchise name of the NHL Ice Hockey team based in Pittsburgh?

2. Can you solve this sporting equation? '35F in the WSCF'

3. In which sport can you win the Sid Waddell Trophy?

4. 'NAN YOWLS JUNE' is an anagram of which Rugby star?

5. In which year did Brazil last win the men's FIFA World Cup?

6. How many competitors are there in an Olympic synchronised swimming team?

7. Jari Litmanen and Heikki Kovalainen have both represented which country?

8. These three sports stars all share parts of their names with board games...

   Luigi **?** (Football)
   Josip **?** (Cycling)
   Rocky **?** (American Football)

# Mystery Guest

**In this round you are given three clues
to a sports star's identity.**

### Who is this Mystery Guest?

1. I have spent over 300 weeks as world number one in my sport.

2. My sister has won seven Grand Slam singles titles, five coming at Wimbledon.

3. In 2019, I became the oldest Grand Slam finalist in the Open Era.

### Who is this Mystery Guest?

1. I was the quickest player to score 3,000 Test runs and take 300 Test wickets.

2. I also played professional football for Scunthorpe United.

3. I held the record for the highest number of Test wickets taken by an Englishman, until James Anderson surpassed me in 2015.

# Home or Away

**In this round there is a choice of a home question
for one point or an away question for two.**

*Do you want a home question on Football for one point or an
away question on Gymnastics for two?*

1. **Football.** Which team won the English First Division in the season
   before it became known as the Premier League?

2. **Gymnastics.** In 2019, which American gymnast won a record 25th
   World Championship medal, by winning gold on the floor?

*Do you want a home question on Golf for one point or an away
question on American Football for two?*

1. **Golf.** Which South African golfer won his last three majors across
   three decades, the 1990s, 2000s and 2010s?

2. **American Football.** Joe Montana won the Super Bowl MVP
   award on three occasions as the winning quarterback of which team?

*Do you want a home question on Rugby Union for one point or an away question on Formula One for two?*

1.  **Rugby Union.** Which England scrum-half became the first player to start for two different Premiership Final-winning teams?

2.  **Formula One.** Since 2019, how many points are awarded for setting the fastest lap in a Formula One Grand Prix?

*Do you want a home question on Cricket for one point or an away question on Boxing for two?*

1.  **Cricket.** In 2019, who surpassed Dennis Lillee to become Australia's third highest wicket taker?

2.  **Boxing.** Which British boxer won an Olympic silver medal in Athens before going on to become WBA light-welterweight champion in 2009?

# Top Ten

**Great Britain won gold in 11 sports at the
London Olympics in 2012. Cycling was
top of the list – what are the other ten?**

There's a point for each one you correctly identify, but guess one
wrong and you lose your points from this round...

1 ............................................................

2 ............................................................

3 ............................................................

4 ............................................................

5 ............................................................

6 ............................................................

7 ............................................................

8 ............................................................

9 ............................................................

10 ............................................................

# Buzzer Round

**The answers to all the questions in this round
begin with the letter C. In the case of a person it's
the surname that will begin with that letter...**

1. Which English racecourse hosts the Gold Cup in March every year?

2. What position in netball allows a player to move anywhere on court except the scoring circles?

3. Which cyclist won the BBC Sports Personality of the Year Award in 2011?

4. What nationality is Snooker World Champion Cliff Thorburn?

5. Which defender scored Arsenal's only goal in the 2006 Champions League Final against Barcelona?

6. Which Belgian woman won four Grand Slam singles titles between 2005 and 2011?

7. The area of a cricket field deep on the batsmen's leg side is typically named what?

8. On which golf course did Francesco Molinari win the Open Championship in 2018?

9. What sport sees players slide stones on ice towards the house?

10. In Rugby League which Super League team are nicknamed the 'Tigers'?

# Sprint Finish

**Describe these ten sporting words
and phrases to your team...**

1. Fairway

2. World Cup

3. Motorbike

4. Warrington Wolves

5. Strawberries and cream

6. Kayaking

7. Joe Calzaghe

8. Final whistle

9. Winter Olympics

10. Sliding tackle

# Game 35 Answers

**One-Minute Round**

1. Penguins; 2. 35 Frames in the World Snooker Championship Final; 3. Darts; 4. Alun Wyn Jones; 5. 2002; 6. Eight; 7. Finland; 8. Luigi MONOPOLI, Josip SKRABL, Rocky CHESS

**Mystery Guest**

Serena Williams, Ian Botham

**Home or Away**

1. Football. Leeds United
2. Gymnastics. Simone Biles

<br>

1. Golf. Ernie Els
2. American Football. San Francisco 49ers

<br>

1. Rugby Union. Richard Wigglesworth
2. Formula One. One

<br>

1. Cricket. Nathan Lyon
2. Boxing. Amir Khan

**Top Ten**

Athletics
Rowing
Boxing
Equestrian
Canoeing
Sailing
Shooting
Taekwondo
Tennis
Triathlon

**Buzzer Round**

1. Cheltenham; 2. Centre; 3. Mark Cavendish; 4. Canadian; 5. Sol Campbell; 6. Kim Clijsters; 7. Cow Corner; 8. Carnoustie; 9. Curling; 10. Castleford

# Game 36

# One-Minute Round

1. Which NBA basketball team play their home games at Madison Square Garden?

2. Can you solve this sporting equation? '25P for a W in FO'

3. In which sport do women compete in the K1, K2 and K4 classes at the Olympics?

4. 'END FAIL' is an anagram of which stadium?

5. In which year did Sandy Lyle win the US Masters?

6. How many teams currently compete across the two County Championship divisions?

7. Brendan Taylor and Peter Ndlovu have both represented which country?

8. These three sports stars all share parts of their names with languages…

   Bruce **?** (Cricket)
   Harris **?** (Golf)
   Peter **?** (Aussie Rules)

# Mystery Guest

**In this round you are given three clues
to a sports star's identity.**

*Who is this Mystery Guest?*

1. I won my first two Olympic medals on the water alongside Andy Holmes.

2. In 2003, I won the Golden Sports Personality of the Year award.

3. I won the last of my five Olympic gold medals in 2000.

*Who is this Mystery Guest?*

1. My England career spanned 13 years, beginning in 1998.

2. At professional club level, I've only ever played for Toulon and Newcastle Falcons.

3. I kicked England to World Cup glory in Australia in 2003.

# Home or Away

**In this round there is a choice of a home question for one point or an away question for two.**

*Do you want a home question on Football for one point or an away question on Cycling for two?*

1. **Football.** Which Irishman scored the first of his 126 Premier League goals in 1999 for Coventry City and the last for Aston Villa in 2012?

2. **Cycling.** Which British cyclist won Olympic Team Pursuit gold in Rio, 12 years after winning Individual Pursuit gold in Athens?

*Do you want a home question on Cricket for one point or an away question on Formula One for two?*

1. **Cricket.** Which Afghanistan bowler became the quickest person to reach the milestone of 100 ODI wickets?

2. **Formula One.** Which Formula One Grand Prix, held on the Baku City Circuit, was raced the first time in 2017?

*Do you want a home question on Golf for one point or an away question on Baseball for two?*

1. **Golf.** In 2018, which American became the first golfer to win back-to-back US Open titles since Curtis Strange?

2. **Baseball.** Which Major League Baseball team have played their home games at Fenway Park since 1912?

*Do you want a home question on Athletics for one point or an away question on Netball for two?*

1. **Athletics.** In 2015, who became only the fifth British athlete to hold Olympic, World, Commonwealth and European titles all at the same time?

2. **Netball.** Which country has reached every Commonwealth Games Final in netball, winning gold on three occasions?

# Top Ten

**Name the ten winners of the Wimbledon Ladies'
Singles title between 1990 and 2010?**

There's a point for each one you correctly identify, but guess one
wrong and you lose your points from this round...

1 ................................................................

2 ................................................................

3 ................................................................

4 ................................................................

5 ................................................................

6 ................................................................

7 ................................................................

8 ................................................................

9 ................................................................

10 ................................................................

# Buzzer Round

**All the questions in this round are about track stars...**

1. Which Asian country has won the most Winter Olympic medals in Short Track Speed Skating?

2. In which sport did Poole Pirates win the Elite League seven times between 2000 and 2015?

3. In horse racing, which track hosts the Melbourne Cup each year?

4. Which Italian rider won the MotoGP World Championship seven times in the 2000s?

5. In which country would you find the Interlagos Formula One track, often known for hosting the penultimate or final race of the season?

6. Rachel Atherton is a multiple World Champion in which sport?

7. What is the last track event of the heptathlon competition?

8. Jason Plato, Matt Neal and Colin Turkington are all champions in which sport?

9. Which Briton won seven Track Cycling World Championship gold medals between 2011 and 2016?

10. Which former Formula One World Champion won the 24 Hours of Le Mans race in 2018?

# Sprint Finish

**Describe these ten sporting words
and phrases to your team...**

1. Deuce

2. Rio Ferdinand

3. Sailing

4. Century

5. Six Nations

6. Long jump

7. Taekwondo

8. Mercedes

9. Formation

10. LA Lakers

# Game 36 Answers

**One-Minute Round**
1. New York Knicks; 2. 25 Points for a Win in Formula One; 3. Kayaking; 4. Anfield;
5. 1988; 6. 18; 7. Zimbabwe; 8. Bruce FRENCH, Harris ENGLISH,
Peter GERMAN

**Mystery Guest**
Steve Redgrave, Jonny Wilkinson

**Home or Away**
1. Football. Robbie Keane
2. Cycling. Bradley Wiggins

1. Cricket. Rashid Khan
2. Formula One. Azerbaijan

1. Golf. Brooks Koepka
2. Baseball. Boston Red Sox

1. Athletics. Greg Rutherford
2. Netball. Australia

**Top Ten**
Martina Navratilova
Steffi Graf
Conchita Martínez
Martina Hingis
Jana Novotná
Lindsay Davenport
Venus Williams
Serena Williams
Maria Sharapova
Amélie Mauresmo

**Buzzer Round**
1. South Korea; 2. Speedway; 3. Flemington; 4. Valentino Rossi; 5. Brazil;
6. Downhill mountain biking; 7. 800m; 8. British Touring Cars; 9. Laura Kenny;
10. Fernando Alonso

# Game 37

# One-Minute Round

1. With which football team do Wasps share the Ricoh Arena?

2. Can you solve this sporting equation? '1P for a FT in B'

3. In which sport do amateurs compete in the Walker Cup?

4. 'ALL BABES' is an anagram of which sport?

5. In which year did Turin host the Winter Olympics?

6. How many different boxing weights did women compete in at the Olympics in Rio?

7. Sabine Lisicki and Marcel Siem have both represented which country?

8. These three sports stars all share parts of their names with words that come before BEE…

   **?** Harrison (Athletics)
   Thomas **?** (Ice Hockey)
   Issac **?** (Football)

# Mystery Guest

**In this round you are given three clues
to a sports star's identity.**

## Who is this Mystery Guest?

1.  I was born in Wiesbaden, West Germany in 1959 but grew up in America.

2.  I won the Davis Cup on five occasions with my wins spanning three decades.

3.  My rivalries with Björn Borg and Jimmy Connors are some of the most well known in the history of tennis.

## Who is this Mystery Guest?

1.  I was born in Belgium but represented Great Britain throughout my career.

2.  I have won five Olympic gold medals and eight World Championship titles.

3.  In 2012, I became the first British winner of the Tour de France.

# Home or Away

**In this round there is a choice of a home question for one point or an away question for two.**

*Do you want a home question on Football for one point or an away question on Rowing for two?*

1. **Football.** Since 1980, which is the only country to win the FIFA World Cup as a host nation?

2. **Rowing.** Which rower won Olympic gold in the men's eight in Rio, having previously won two gold medals in the Coxless Four?

*Do you want a home question on Cricket for one point or an away question on Formula One for two?*

1. **Cricket.** Who is Sri Lanka's leading run scorer in Tests, amassing over 12,000 runs before retiring from international cricket in 2015?

2. **Formula One.** Who won the F1 Driver's World Championship in 2016, 34 years after his father won the title?

*Do you want a home question on Golf for one point or an away question on Darts for two?*

1. **Golf.** In 2010, which Northern Irishman became the first European to win the US Open since Tony Jacklin in 1970?

2. **Darts.** Which Australian darts player has lost in the final of both the BDO and PDC World Championships?

*Do you want a home question on Rugby Union for one point or an away question on Baseball for two?*

1. **Rugby Union.** Which Welsh forward won both his first cap and his 100th and last cap for Wales against the Barbarians?

2. **Baseball.** Which Major League Baseball team's franchise name comes last alphabetically?

# Top Ten

**Name the ten cities that have hosted the
Commonwealth Games since 1980?**

There's a point for each one you correctly identify, but guess one
wrong and you lose your points from this round…

1 ............................................................................

2 ............................................................................

3 ............................................................................

4 ............................................................................

5 ............................................................................

6 ............................................................................

7 ............................................................................

8 ............................................................................

9 ............................................................................

10 ............................................................................

# Buzzer Round

**All the questions in this round are about South America
and sports stars from that continent…**

1. In 2019, which South American country won only their third Rugby Union World Cup match, defeating Fiji 30-27?

2. Which major did golfer Ángel Cabrera win in 2009?

3. Paraguayan footballer Roque Santa Cruz played in the Premier League for Blackburn Rovers and which other club?

4. Caterine Ibargüen won Olympic gold for Colombia in 2016, in which field event?

5. Which is the only country in mainland South America that has hosted Test cricket?

6. Which Chilean tennis player reached men's world number one in 1998?

7. Colombian Nairo Quintana won which of cycling's Grand Tour events in 2016?

8. In 2019, which Brazilian footballer became the all-time leading scorer at the Women's World Cup?

9. In 2012, which Venezuelan Williams driver won his only Formula One Grand Prix?

10. Which country has won the most Summer Olympic medals in Beach Volleyball?

# Sprint Finish

**Describe these ten sporting words
and phrases to your team...**

1. Headingley

2. Cue ball

3. Hat-trick

4. London Marathon

5. Dummy

6. Umpire

7. Challenge Cup

8. Denise Lewis

9. In the rough

10. Phil Tufnell

# Game 37 Answers

### One-Minute Round
1. Coventry City; 2. 1 Point for a Free Throw in Basketball; 3. Golf; 4. Baseball; 5. 2006; 6. Three; 7. Germany; 8. QUEEN Harrison, Thomas SPELLING, Issac HONEY

### Mystery Guest
John McEnroe, Bradley Wiggins

### Home or Away
1. Football. France
2. Rowing. Andrew Triggs Hodge

1. Cricket. Kumar Sangakkara
2. Formula One. Nico Rosberg

1. Golf. Graeme McDowell
2. Darts. Simon Whitlock

1. Rugby Union. Martyn Williams
2. Baseball. New York Yankees

### Top Ten
Brisbane
Edinburgh
Auckland
Victoria
Kuala Lumpur
Manchester
Melbourne
Delhi
Glasgow
Gold Coast

### Buzzer Round
1. Uruguay; 2. US Masters; 3. Manchester City; 4. Triple jump; 5. Guyana; 6. Marcelo Ríos; 7. Vuelta a España; 8. Marta; 9. Pastor Maldonado; 10. Brazil

# Game 38

# One-Minute Round

1. Which American football team play their home games in the NFL at the Superdome?

2. Can you solve this sporting equation? '23 GM for MP at the OG'

3. In which sport might you find a bunny and a golden duck?

4. 'MARTINIS HASHED' is an anagram of which British athletics star?

5. In which year did England win the men's football World Cup?

6. How many minutes in the sin bin does a player get for a yellow card in Rugby Union?

7. Lilly King and Lolo Jones have both represented which country at the Olympics?

8. These three sports stars all share parts of their names with places you might go for a picnic...

   Walter **?** (American Football)
   Inbee **?** (Golf)
   Craig **?** (Football)

# Mystery Guest

**In this round you are given three clues
to a sports star's identity.**

## Who is this Mystery Guest?

1.  I scored a hat-trick in my first El Clásico in the Nou Camp.

2.  I have scored over 600 goals for my club since I made my debut
    in 2004.

3.  I am the all-time top goal scorer for Argentina.

## Who is this Mystery Guest?

1.  I won a Commonwealth medal for England as a 17-year-old in 2010.

2.  I was one of only four people to win multiple Olympic gold medals
    for Great Britain in Rio.

3.  As of 2019, I am Britain's most successful male artistic gymnast
    in history.

# Home or Away

In this round there is a choice of a home question
for one point or an away question for two.

*Do you want a home question on Athletics for one point or an
away question on Rugby League for two?*

1. **Athletics.** Who ran the final leg for Great Britain as they won gold
   in the World Championship 4x400m relay final in 1991?

2. **Rugby League.** Which Australian side won the World Club
   Challenge in 2014, 2019 and 2020?

*Do you want a home question on Cricket for one point or an away
question on Swimming for two?*

1. **Cricket.** In 2007, who surpassed Ian Healy's record for most
   dismissals for a wicket keeper in Tests, ending his career with
   over 500?

2. **Swimming.** Adam Peaty became Britain's first Olympic 100m
   breaststroke champion since which swimmer won gold in 1988?

*Do you want a home question on Tennis for one point or an away question on Basketball for two?*

1. **Tennis.** Who won all seven of his Wimbledon singles finals over an eight-year period, defeating Goran Ivanišević in two of them?

2. **Basketball.** Which NBA basketball team's franchise name comes first alphabetically?

*Do you want a home question on Football for one point or an away question on the Winter Olympics for two?*

1. **Football.** In October 2019, who became only the second team in Premier League history to win a game 9-0 with their victory against Southampton?

2. **Winter Olympics.** In 2014, which city hosted its first F1 Grand Prix in the same year that it hosted the Winter Olympics?

# Top Ten

**Name the first ten different golfers to
hold the position of World Number One
since the rankings were introduced in 1986.**

There's a point for each one you correctly identify, but guess one
wrong and you lose your points from this round...

1 ................................................................

2 ................................................................

3 ................................................................

4 ................................................................

5 ................................................................

6 ................................................................

7 ................................................................

8 ................................................................

9 ................................................................

10 ................................................................

# Buzzer Round

**The answers to all the questions in this round
begin with the letter R. In the case of a person
it's the surname that will begin with that letter...**

1. In which biannual golf event do Europe compete against the USA?

2. What nationality is Grand Slam tennis champion Simona Halep?

3. In 2015, New Zealand fly-half Dan Carter signed for which French Rugby club?

4. Which snooker player won six World Championships in the 1970s?

5. Which jockey rode Tiger Roll to Grand National victories in 2018 and 2019?

6. Who are the only football team beginning with the letter R to play in the Premier League?

7. Which team from Toronto won the 2019 NBA Championship?

8. In cricket, what type of dismissal is it when a fielder hits the stumps with a batsman out of his crease?

9. Which British woman has won the London Marathon on three occasions?

10. Which gymnastic discipline involves items such as a ball and ribbon?

# Sprint Finish

**Describe these ten sporting words
and phrases to your team...**

1. Green jacket

2. Double top

3. Stephen Hendry

4. Euro 96

5. Ski Sunday

6. Clean and jerk

7. New York Giants

8. Vault

9. Own goal

10. Brownlee Brothers

# Game **38** Answers

## One-Minute Round
1. New Orleans; 2. 23 Gold Medals for Michael Phelps at the Olympic Games;
3. Cricket; 4. Dina Asher-Smith; 5. 1966; 6. Ten; 7. USA; 8. Walter BEACH,
Inbee PARK, Craig FORREST

## Mystery Guest
Lionel Messi, Max Whitlock

## Home or Away
1.  Athletics. Kriss Akabusi
2.  Rugby League. Sydney Roosters

1.  Cricket. Mark Boucher
2.  Swimming. Adrian Moorhouse

1.  Tennis. Pete Sampras
2.  Basketball. Milwaukee Bucks

1.  Football. Leicester City
2.  Winter Olympics. Sochi

## Top Ten
Bernhard Langer
Seve Ballesteros
Greg Norman
Nick Faldo
Ian Woosnam
Fred Couples
Nick Price
Tom Lehman
Tiger Woods
Ernie Els

## Buzzer Round
1. Ryder Cup; 2. Romanian; 3. Racing 92; 4. Ray Reardon; 5. Davy Russell;
6. Reading; 7. Raptors; 8. Run out; 9. Paula Radcliffe; 10. Rhythmic

# Game 39

# One-Minute Round

1. Where do Scotland play their home games in the Six Nations?

2. Can you solve this sporting equation? '10E in a D'

3. In which sport is the Musketeers' Trophy won each year by a man in Paris?

4. 'BRITS FRAMED GOD' is an anagram of which football stadium?

5. In which year did Glasgow host the Commonwealth Games?

6. Over how many metres is an Olympic steeplechase race?

7. Ana Ivanović and Nemanja Vidiić have both represented which country?

8. These three sports stars all share parts of their names with musical instruments…

   Steve **?** (Baseball)
   **?** Dokur (Ice Hockey)
   Sebastien **?** (Archery)

# Mystery Guest

**In this round you are given three clues
to a sports star's identity.**

### *Who is this Mystery Guest?*

1. I received a marriage proposal from a member of the crowd at Wimbledon.

2. In 1988, I won all four Grand Slam titles and Olympic gold in the same year.

3. In 2017, Serena Williams overtook my Open Era record of 22 Grand Slam singles titles.

### *Who is this Mystery Guest?*

1. I am an Olympic, Commonwealth, World and European champion.

2. I won the BBC Sports Personality of the Year award in 1995.

3. At the World Championships in Gothenburg, I broke the men's triple jump world record.

# Home or Away

**In this round there is a choice of a home question
for one point or an away question for two.**

*Do you want a home question on Golf for one point or an away
question on the Winter Olympics for two?*

1.  **Golf.** In 2016, Danny Willett and which other European golfer won
    their first Major Championship?

2.  **Winter Olympics.** Which country, that has hosted the Games on
    two occasions, top the all-time Winter Olympic medal table?

*Do you want a home question on Tennis for one point or an away
question on Gymnastics for two?*

1.  **Tennis.** In 1985, which 17-year-old became the first unseeded player
    to win the Wimbledon Men's Singles title in the open era?

2.  **Gymnastics.** In 2018, which gymnast helped England retain their
    men's team Commonwealth title, before winning individual All
    Around gold for the first time?

*Do you want a home question on Rugby Union for one point or an away question on Formula One for two?*

1. **Rugby Union.** Which South African was the 2011 World Cup top points scorer despite his team only winning four games?

2. **Formula One.** Which team have won a record number of Formula One Constructors' Championships?

*Do you want a home question on Football for one point or an away question on Snooker for two?*

1. **Football.** Which midfielder scored in the final as Liverpool were crowned domestic European Champions in 2005, before featuring in the final as his country became European Champions in 2008?

2. **Snooker.** Who was the only player to beat Stephen Hendry in a won World Snooker Championship Final in the 1990s?

# Top Ten

**Eoin Morgan captained England to
World Cup victory in 2019; name the
other ten players in the team that day.**

There's a point for each one you correctly identify, but guess one
wrong and you lose your points from this round…

1  .............................................................................

2  .............................................................................

3  .............................................................................

4  .............................................................................

5  .............................................................................

6  .............................................................................

7  .............................................................................

8  .............................................................................

9  .............................................................................

10 .............................................................................

# Buzzer Round

**All the questions in this round are about the
USA and sports stars from that country...**

1. Where is the US Open tennis tournament held?

2. Basketball star LeBron James started his NBA career with
   which team?

3. In 2019, which woman became the most successful athlete in World
   Championship history?

4. Bill Belichick has won a record number of Super Bowls with which
   American Football team?

5. Lindsey Vonn is an Olympic and World Champion for the USA in
   which winter sport?

6. Which boxer defeated Muhammad Ali in 1971, in a contest billed as
   'Fight of the Century'?

7. Who is the highest scoring American in English Premier League
   history?

8. In which sport do the Avalanche and the Redwings compete?

9. Which golfer has made the most appearances for the USA at the
   Ryder Cup, first doing so in 1995?

10. Which American swimmer is the most successful Olympian of all
    time, winning a total of 23 gold medals?

# Sprint Finish

**Describe these ten sporting words
and phrases to your team...**

1. The Crucible

2. Backhand

3. Martin Johnson

4. Real Madrid

5. Fosbury Flop

6. Beach volleyball

7. G-force

8. Swimming pool

9. Darts

10. Early retirement

# Game 39 Answers

**One-Minute Round**
1. Murrayfield; 2. 10 Events in a Decathlon; 3. Tennis; 4. Stamford Bridge; 5. 2014; 6. 3,000; 7. Serbia; 8. Steve SAX, TUBA Dokur, Sebastien FLUTE

**Mystery Guest**
Steffi Graf, Jonathan Edwards

**Home or Away**
1. Golf. Henrik Stenson
2. Winter Olympics. Norway

1. Tennis. Boris Becker
2. Gymnastics. Nile Wilson

1. Rugby Union. Morné Steyn
2. Formula One. Ferrari

1. Football. Xabi Alonso
2. Snooker. Ken Doherty

**Top Ten**
Jason Roy
Jonny Bairstow
Joe Root
Ben Stokes
Jos Buttler
Chris Woakes
Liam Plunkett
Jofra Archer
Adil Rashid
Mark Wood

**Buzzer Round**
1. Flushing Meadows; 2. Cleveland Cavaliers; 3. Allyson Felix; 4. New England Patriots; 5. Alpine skiing; 6. Joe Frazier; 7. Clint Dempsey; 8. Ice hockey; 9. Phil Mickelson; 10. Michael Phelps

# Game 40

# One-Minute Round

1. In which country is the cricket ground Eden Gardens?

2. Can you solve this sporting equation? '40R in the GN'

3. In which sport do teams compete for the World Series?

4. 'ANORAKS SELLS GLEE' is an anagram of which Basketball team?

5. In which year did Ronnie O'Sullivan record a 147 in less than six minutes at the Crucible?

6. How many majors are there on the Women's LPGA Tour?

7. Hakan Şükür and Muzzy Izzet have both played international football for which country?

8. These three sports stars all share parts of their names with English counties...

   **?** Malcolm (Cricket)
   Matt **?** (Football)
   Peter **?** (Tennis)

# Mystery Guest

**In this round you are given three clues to a sports star's identity.**

### *Who is this Mystery Guest?*

1. My real name is Eldrick, though I have achieved my success under a different name.

2. I have been World Number One in my sport for over 680 weeks.

3  In 2019, I won my first major for 11 years.

### *Who is this Mystery Guest?*

1. I have scored in a World Cup Final.

2. I won the Champions League title in 2002, with Real Madrid.

3. As of 2020, I am the only manager to have won the European Cup three times in a row.

# Home or Away

**In this round there is a choice of a home question for one point or an away question for two.**

*Do you want a home question on Football. for one point or an away question on Swimming for two?*

1. **Football.** In 2015, which Southampton player broke Robbie Fowler's record for the quickest Premier League hat-trick?

2. **Swimming.** Who won Great Britain's only Olympic swimming gold in Rio by breaking their own World Record in the final?

*Do you want a home question on Tennis for one point or an away question on Rugby League for two?*

1. **Tennis.** Which player from Argentina reached his second US Open final in 2018, nine years after winning his first?

2. **Rugby League.** Which franchise name is shared by Rugby League teams from Brisbane and London?

*Do you want a home question on Golf for one point or an away question on the Winter Olympics for two?*

1. **Golf.** Which British golfer won the Open Championship in 1985 and the US Masters in 1988?

2. **Winter Olympics.** Which European country has hosted the Winter Olympics on three occasions, most recently in 1992?

*Do you want a home question on Rugby Union for one point or an away question on Horse Racing for two?*

1. **Rugby Union.** In 2006, which England player became the first person to win both Rugby Union's Guinness Premiership and Rugby League's Super League titles?

2. **Horse Racing.** Which racecourse hosts the English Classics the 1000 and 2000 Guineas?

# Top Ten

**Name the top ten countries in the medal table
at the 2019 World Athletics Championships.**

There's a point for each one you correctly identify, but guess one
wrong and you lose your points from this round…

1  .......................................................................

2  .......................................................................

3  .......................................................................

4  .......................................................................

5  .......................................................................

6  .......................................................................

7  .......................................................................

8  .......................................................................

9  .......................................................................

10  ......................................................................

# Buzzer Round

1. The White Sox play their Major League Baseball home games in which city?

2. Who scored six goals for the Lionesses at the 2019 Women's World Cup?

3. Who did Jimmy White lose to on four occasions in snooker's World Championship Final?

4. The white flag is used in MotoGP to warn racers of what?

5. What was the name of the stadium that hosted athletics at the 1908 Olympics in London?

6. Jake White coached which country to victory in the 2007 Rugby World Cup Final?

7. In the Tour de France, the white jersey is awarded to which rider?

8. In which sport did Shaun White win three Winter Olympic gold medals?

9. Which county did England all-rounder Craig White play first-class cricket for between 1990 and 2007?

10. The All Whites is the nickname of which international football team?

# Sprint Finish

**Describe these ten sporting words
and phrases to your team...**

1. Golden State Warriors

2. Balance beam

3. Jürgen Klopp

4. Knock on

5. Southpaw

6. Press conference

7. Long pot

8. Beth Tweddle

9. Mobot

10. Step over

# Game 40 Answers

## One-Minute Round
1. India; 2. 40 Runners in the Grand National; 3. Baseball; 4. Los Angeles Lakers; 5. 1997; 6. Five; 7. Turkey; 8. DEVON Malcolm, Matt DERBYSHIRE, Peter NORFOLK

## Mystery Guest
Tiger Woods, Zinedine Zidane

## Home or Away
1.  Football. Sadio Mané
2.  Swimming. Adam Peaty

1.  Tennis. Juan Martín del Potro
2.  Rugby League. Broncos

1.  Golf. Sandy Lyle
2.  Winter Olympics. France

1.  Rugby Union. Jason Robinson
2.  Horse Racing. Newmarket

## Top Ten
USA
Kenya
Jamaica
China
Ethiopia
Great Britain
Germany
Japan
Netherlands
Uganda

## Buzzer Round
1. Chicago; 2. Ellen White; 3. Stephen Hendry; 4. Rain; 5. White City; 6. South Africa; 7. Best Young Rider; 8. Snowboarding; 9. Yorkshire; 10. New Zealand

# Game 41

# One-Minute Round

1. Which American racecourse hosts the Kentucky Derby?

2. Can you solve this sporting equation? '26 = M in a M'

3. In which sport can you be awarded the Harry Sunderland trophy?

4. 'KEY CHIOICE' is an anagram of which sport?

5. In which year did Andy Murray win his first Wimbledon title?

6. How many different weights were contested in the men's Olympic boxing competition in Rio?

7. Becky James and Jamie Donaldson have both represented which country?

8. These three sports stars all share parts of their names with things you might associate with fishing...

   Jay **?** (Baseball)
   **?** Hussain (Boxing)
   **?** Pampling (Golf)

# Mystery Guest

**In this round you are given three clues
to a sports star's identity.**

### Who is this Mystery Guest?

1. I'm a former tennis player, born in Prague in 1956.

2. I won nine Wimbledon singles titles, my last coming against Zina Garrison.

3. I have won a total of 59 Grand Slam titles in my career.

### Who is this Mystery Guest?

1. In 2006, I ran the 5000 metres in a time of 13 minutes 9.40 seconds. This was the second fastest time by a British athlete.

2. I won my first Olympic gold medal in 2012.

3. After the 2017 World Championships, I switched my focus to running marathons.

# Home or Away

**In this round there is a choice of a home question
for one point or an away question for two.**

*Do you want a home question on Football for one point or an
away question on Rugby League for two?*

1. **Football.** In 2020, who overtook Thierry Henry to become the
   leading overseas goal scorer in Premier League history?

2. **Rugby League.** In 2017, which Rugby League team finished top of
   the league for the first time in their 91-year history?

*Do you want a home question on Tennis for one point or an away
question on Horse Racing for two?*

1. **Tennis.** Which Brazilian is the only player since 1990 to have
   reached three or more Grand Slam singles finals and won them all?

2. **Horse Racing.** Which racecourse hosts the King George VI chase,
   traditionally held on Boxing Day?

*Do you want a home question on Golf for one point or an away question on British Sport for two?*

1.  **Golf.** The Men's World Golf rankings were introduced in 1986; which European two-time major winner was the first to top them?

2.  **British Sport.** Which famous race is 4 miles and 374 yards long and starts in Putney and ends in Mortlake?

*Do you want a home question on Athletics for one point or an away question on Baseball for two?*

1.  **Athletics.** At the Olympics, discus and which other field event are included in the decathlon but not the heptathlon?

2.  **Baseball.** Which Major League Baseball team's franchise name comes first alphabetically?

# Top Ten

**Name the ten Formula One drivers that
have won the most Grand Prix races as
of the end of the 2019 season.**

There's a point for each one you correctly identify, but guess one
wrong and you lose your points from this round…

1 .............................................................

2 .............................................................

3 .............................................................

4 .............................................................

5 .............................................................

6 .............................................................

7 .............................................................

8 .............................................................

9 .............................................................

10 ............................................................

# Buzzer Round

**All the questions in this round are about New Zealand
and sports stars from that country...**

1. Who captained New Zealand to Rugby Union World Cup Final victory on home soil in 2011?

2. Hamish Bond and Eric Murray are double Olympic champions in which sport?

3. With which team did defender Ryan Nelsen make his Premier League debut?

4. Golfer Lydia Ko won Olympic silver at which games?

5. Which New Zealand boxer held the WBO Heavyweight title between 2016 and 2018?

6. New Zealand Paralympian Liam Malone won silver behind which British sprinter in the 100m at Rio 2016?

7. Which bowler has taken the most Test wickets for New Zealand?

8. Which New Zealand Equestrian rider won back to back Olympic gold medals on Charisma?

9. Which country did New Zealand beat in the final of the 2019 Netball World Cup?

10. In which sport has Benji Marshall captained New Zealand more times than anyone else?

# Sprint Finish

**Describe these ten sporting words
and phrases to your team...**

1. Middle pocket

2. Olympic Village

3. Three-pointer

4. Sand wedge

5. Rings

6. Brian Lara

7. Leinster

8. Zonal marking

9. Mark Cavendish

10. The Chair

# Game 41 Answers

**One-Minute Round**
1. Churchill Downs; 2. 26 = Miles in a Marathon; 3. Rugby League; 4. Ice Hockey; 5. 2013; 6. Ten; 7. Wales; 8. Jay HOOK, BAIT Hussain, ROD Pampling

**Mystery Guest**
Martina Navratilova, Mo Farah

**Home or Away**
1.  Football. Sergio Agüero
2.  Rugby League. Castleford Tigers

1.  Tennis. Gustavo Kuerten
2.  Horse Racing. Kempton Park

1.  Golf. Bernhard Langer
2.  British Sport. Boat Race

1.  Athletics. Pole vault
2.  Baseball. Los Angeles Angels

**Top Ten**
Michael Schumacher
Lewis Hamilton
Sebastian Vettel
Alain Prost
Ayrton Senna
Fernando Alonso
Nigel Mansell
Jackie Stewart
Jim Clark
Niki Lauda

**Buzzer Round**
1. Richie McCaw; 2. Rowing; 3. Blackburn Rovers; 4. Rio 2016; 5. Joseph Parker; 6. Jonnie Peacock; 7. Richard Hadlee; 8. Mark Todd; 9. Australia; 10. Rugby League

# Game 42

# One-Minute Round

1. Which casino hosted the rematch between Deontay Wilder and Tyson Fury in 2020?

2. Can you solve this sporting equation? '5P on a BT'

3. In which sport might a competitor perform a salchow?

4. 'CRICKET PAL' is an anagram of which football stadium?

5. In which year was Zara Phillips named BBC Sports Personality of the Year?

6. To the nearest metre, how long was the men's Triple Jump World Record set by Jonathan Edwards?

7. Àlex Correjta and Carlos Moyá both represented which country in the Davis Cup?

8. These three sports stars all share parts of their names with types of bad weather…

   Rodrigo **?** (Football)
   John **?** (Cricket)
   **?** Johnson (American Football)

# Mystery Guest

**In this round you are given three clues
to a sports star's identity.**

### Who is this Mystery Guest?

1. I represented Canada at the Olympics in Seoul, where I won gold.

2. I had a brief cameo in the blockbuster film *Ocean's Eleven*.

3. I finished my professional career with a 41-2-1 record, my only draw coming against Evander Holyfield in 1999.

### Who is this Mystery Guest?

1. I made my club debut in 1999 at the age of 20.

2. In 2009, I captained my country to its first Six Nations Grand Slam in 61 years.

3. I hold the Irish record for the most international tries scored.

# Home or Away

**In this round there is a choice of a home question
for one point or an away question for two.**

*Do you want a home question on Football for one point or an
away question on Horse Racing for two?*

1.  **Football.** Which Welshman has played in four FA Cup finals since
    2000, scoring the winning goal in two of them?

2.  **Horse Racing.** Which horse did Bob Champion ride to victory in
    the Grand National at Aintree?

*Do you want a home question on Cricket for one point or an away
question on Formula One for two?*

1.  **Cricket.** Which cricketer has scored over 7,000 runs for England in
    one-day internationals, and at the 2019 World Cup hit a record 17
    sixes against Afghanistan?

2.  **Formula One.** In 2009, who became the first driver from his
    country to win a Formula One Grand Prix since Alan Jones in 1981?

*Do you want a home question on Golf for one point or an away question on Commonwealth Games for two?*

1. **Golf.** Thomas Bjørn became the first player from which country to both represent and captain Europe at the Ryder Cup?

2. **Commonwealth Games.** Which sport was first introduced to the Commonwealth Games in 1998, with the current singles champions being James Willstrop and Joelle King?

*Do you want a home question on Tennis for one point or an away question on Rugby League for two?*

1. **Tennis.** Who, at the 2018 Australian Open, became only the sixth British man to reach a Grand Slam singles semi-final in the Open Era?

2. **Rugby League.** Which team reached the Super League Grand Final four times between 2010 and 2019, losing them all?

# Top Ten

**The USA have reached the semi-finals at
every Women's Football World Cup; name the
other ten countries that have played in a semi-final.**

There's a point for each one you correctly identify, but guess one
wrong and you lose your points from this round...

1 .................................................................

2 .................................................................

3 .................................................................

4 .................................................................

5 .................................................................

6 .................................................................

7 .................................................................

8 .................................................................

9 .................................................................

10 ................................................................

# Buzzer Round

**The answers to all the questions in this round begin with the letter B. In the case of a person it's the surname that will begin with that letter...**

1. The Bulls play rugby league in which Yorkshire city?

2. Which circuit held the Formula One British Grand Prix on 12 occasions between 1964 and 1986?

3. Which European golfer won the Open Championship on three occasions between 1979 and 1988?

4. What is the franchise name of the NFL team that Tom Brady joined after leaving the New England Patriots?

5. Which Englishman won the World Snooker Championship in 2015?

6. Which team beginning with B were relegated at the end of their only season in the Premier League in 1998?

7. Who captained Australia to victory in the 1987 Cricket World Cup?

8. Which Australian won the women's French Open singles title in 2019?

9. In what sport would find a pitcher, a mound and a short stop?

10. Which All Black was named Rugby World Player of the Year in 2016 and 2017?

# Sprint Finish

**Describe these ten sporting words
and phrases to your team...**

1.  Giant slalom

2.  Middlesex

3.  Paula Radcliffe

4.  Fixture list

5.  Early bath

6.  Birdie

7.  Footwork

8.  Billiards

9.  Goal attack

10. Free agent

# Game 42 Answers

**One-Minute Round**
1. MGM Grand; 2. 5 Players on a Basketball Team; 3. Figure skating; 4. Celtic Park; 5. 2006; 6. 18m; 7. Spain; 8. Rodrigo RAIN, John SNOW, STORM Johnson

**Mystery Guest**
Lennox Lewis, Brian O'Driscoll

**Home or Away**
1. Football. Aaron Ramsey
2. Horse Racing. Aldaniti

1. Cricket. Eoin Morgan
2. Formula One. Mark Webber

1. Golf. Denmark
2. Commonwealth Games. Squash

1. Tennis. Kyle Edmund
2. Rugby League. Warrington Wolves

**Top Ten**
Brazil
Canada
China
England
France
Germany
Japan
Netherlands
Norway
Sweden

**Buzzer Round**
1. Bradford; 2. Brands Hatch; 3. Seve Ballesteros; 4. Buccaneers; 5. Stuart Bingham; 6. Barnsley; 7. Allan Border; 8. Ashleigh Barty; 9. Baseball; 10. Beauden Barrett

# Game 43

# One-Minute Round

1. Ireland play their home Rugby Union games in which stadium?

2. Can you solve this sporting equation? '260PLG for AS'

3. Which of golf's majors features a par 3 contest on the Wednesday before it starts?

4. 'JAILED MONARCH' is an anagram of which basketball star?

5. In which year did Steve Redgrave win his fifth Olympic gold medal?

6. What is the minimum number of points needed to win a game of table tennis at the Olympics?

7. For which country have Tirunesh Dibaba and Kenenisa Bekele won Olympic gold medals on the track?

8. These three sports stars all share parts of their names with British Prime Ministers...

   Clive **?** (Rugby League)
   **?** White (Cricket)
   Jay **?** (Motor Racing)

# Mystery Guest

**In this round you are given three clues
to a sports star's identity.**

*Who is this Mystery Guest?*

1.  David Beckham broke my caps record for an England outfield player.

2.  I made 646 appearances for West Ham United in my career, scoring 27 goals.

3.  I captained England to World Cup glory in 1966.

*Who is this Mystery Guest?*

1.  I competed in my home Olympics in 2012, at the age of 19.

2.  I set a British women's high jump record of 1.98 metres in August 2016.

3.  I won World Championship gold in the heptathlon in 2019.

# Home or Away

**In this round there is a choice of a home question for one point or an away question for two.**

*Do you want a home question on Rugby Union for one point or an away question on Horse Racing for two?*

1. **Rugby Union.** Who scored a record five drop goals for South Africa in the 1999 World Cup quarter-final against England?

2. **Horse Racing.** Brian Fletcher rode Red Rum to his first two Grand National victories but which jockey rode him when he won the race for a third time in 1977?

*Do you want a home question on Tennis for one point or an away question on Darts for two?*

1. **Tennis.** Which British tennis player reached the US Open Final in 1997, losing to Pat Rafter?

2. **Darts.** Which Englishman became the first player to win both the BDO and PDC World Darts Championships, beating Eric Bristow and Phil Taylor respectively?

*Do you want a home question on Golf for one point or an away question on Winter Sports for two?*

1.  **Golf.** Which American left-handed golfer won the Masters title in 2012 and 2014?

2.  **Winter Sports.** By winning gold in 2009, Nicola Minichiello and Gillian Cooke became Britain's first World Champions since 1965 in which winter sport?

*Do you want a home question on Football for one point or an away question on Sailing for two?*

1.  **Football.** Which Dutchman led the Netherlands and South Korea to back-to-back World Cup Semi-Finals as well as taking Russia to the semi-finals of the Euros in 2008?

2.  **Sailing.** Having started in 1839, the Grand Challenge Cup is the oldest of all races at which annual event?

# Top Ten

**Name the ten basketball teams to have
won the NBA Finals on more than one
occasion as of the start of 2020.**

There's a point for each one you correctly identify, but guess one
wrong and you lose your points from this round…

1 .................................................................................

2 .................................................................................

3 .................................................................................

4 .................................................................................

5 .................................................................................

6 .................................................................................

7 .................................................................................

8 .................................................................................

9 .................................................................................

10 ...............................................................................

# Buzzer Round

**All the questions in this round are about the 2016 Summer Olympics in Rio...**

1. Which sport featured in Rio for the first time since 1904?

2. Which American at Rio 2016 was the first female gymnast to win four gold medals at a single Olympics since 1984?

3. In which indoor and outdoor sport did hosts Brazil win more than one gold medal?

4. For which country did Jack Sock and Bethanie Mattek-Sands win tennis mixed doubles gold?

5. Which British cyclist won three gold medals at the Games?

6. Which famous stadium hosted both football gold medal matches?

7. Which Olympic sport featured at Rio 2016 is last alphabetically?

8. Which South African broke the men's 400m World Record on the way to winning gold?

9. Which British boxer retained her Olympic title in Rio?

10. In which sport did Sarah Sjöström and Mack Horton win Olympic gold?

# Sprint Finish

**Describe these ten sporting words
and phrases to your team...**

1. End zone

2. V.A.R.

3. Points decision

4. Huddersfield Giants

5. Slower ball

6. Rafael Nadal

7. Eagle

8. Strike

9. Everton

10. Huddle

# Game 43 Answers

**One-Minute Round**

1. Aviva Stadium; 2. 260 Premier League Goals for Alan Shearer; 3. US Masters; 4. Michael Jordan; 5. 2000; 6. 11; 7. Ethiopia; 8. Clive CHURCHILL, CAMERON White, Jay CHAMBERLAIN

**Mystery Guest**

Bobby Moore, Katarina Johnson-Thompson

**Home or Away**

1. Rugby Union. Jannie de Beer
2. Horse Racing. Tommy Stack

1. Tennis. Greg Rusedski
2. Darts. Dennis Priestley

1. Golf. Bubba Watson
2. Winter Sports. Bobsleigh

1. Football. Guus Hiddink
2. Sailing. Henley Regatta

**Top Ten**

Boston Celtics
LA Lakers
Chicago Bulls
Golden State Warriors
San Antonio Spurs
Philadelphia 76ers
Detroit Pistons
Miami Heat
New York Knicks
Houston Rockets

**Buzzer Round**

1. Golf; 2. Simone Biles; 3. Volleyball; 4. USA; 5. Jason Kenny; 6. Maracanã; 7. Wrestling; 8. Wayde van Niekerk; 9. Nicola Adams; 10. Swimming

# Game 44

# One-Minute Round

1. Which Australian venue hosts the Boxing Day Test each year?

2. Can you solve this sporting equation? '3E in a T'

3. In which sport might you play on Suzanne Lenglen or Arthur Ashe?

4. 'YEW OR ANYONE' is an anagram of which footballer?

5. In which year were the Commonwealth Games held in Asia for the first time?

6. How many players are there on a Baseball team?

7. Gylfi Sigurðsson and Eiður Guðjohnsen have both played international football for which country?

8. These three sports stars all share parts of their names with types of metal...

   Terrance ? (American Football)
   Tun ? (Boxing)
   Arielle ? (Snowboarding)

# Mystery Guest

**In this round you are given three clues
to a sports star's identity.**

### Who is this Mystery Guest?

1. As of 2019, I have recorded the highest number of Formula One Grand Prix wins.

2. My brother also drove in the sport, most notably for Williams.

3. My seventh and final Formula One World Championship came in 2004.

### Who is this Mystery Guest?

1. My uncle played over 50 times for the Spanish national football team.

2. In 2010, I completed the singles career Golden Slam.

3. As of the end of 2019, Robin Söderling and Novak Djokovic are the only people to beat me at the French Open.

# Home or Away

**In this round there is a choice of a home question
for one point or an away question for two.**

*Do you want a home question on Football for one point or an
away question on Snooker for two?*

1.  **Football.** Since 2016, which Manchester United striker scored on
    his Premier League, Europa League, Champions League and
    England debuts?

2.  **Snooker.** As of the start of 2020, who is the only player to
    reach world number one that hasn't won the World Snooker
    Championship?

*Do you want a home question on Athletics for one point or an
away question on Boxing for two?*

1.  **Athletics.** Which event did Welshman Steve Jones win in London,
    New York and Chicago during the 1980s?

2.  **Boxing.** Which British boxer did Carl Froch beat in 2013 and 2014
    to retain his World Super Middleweight title?

*Do you want a home question on Cricket for one point or an away question on Rugby League for two?*

1. **Cricket.** In 2019, which Australian became the first batsman to register ten successive scores of 50 or more against a single opponent in Test history?

2. **Rugby League.** With which team did Tom Briscoe become the first player ever to score five tries in a Challenge Cup Final?

*Do you want a home question on Tennis for one point or an away question on Motor Racing for two?*

1. **Tennis.** Which country won the Davis Cup in 2019, their sixth title since 2000?

2. **Motor Racing.** In 2019, Jamie Chadwick became the first woman to win which inaugural tournament?

# Top Ten

**Name the ten sports that the USA have
won more than 20 gold medals in at
the Summer Olympics as of 2020?**

There's a point for each one you correctly identify, but guess one
wrong and you lose your points from this round…

1 ............................................................

2 ............................................................

3 ............................................................

4 ............................................................

5 ............................................................

6 ............................................................

7 ............................................................

8 ............................................................

9 ............................................................

10 ............................................................

# Buzzer Round

**All the questions in this round are about Northern Ireland and sports stars from that country...**

1. In 2015, who became the first Northern Irish rider to win the Superbike World Championship?

2. Which is the only Northern Irish Rugby Union team that play in the Pro14?

3. On which apparatus did gymnast Rhys McClenaghan win 2018 Commonwealth gold ahead of Max Whitlock?

4. Who won Pentathlon gold for Great Britain at the 1972 Olympics?

5. In which year did Tony McCoy win the BBC Sports Personality of the Year Award?

6. At which golf course was the 2019 Open Championship held?

7. Which of the home nations beat Northern Ireland in the knockout stages of Euro 2016?

8. Which boxer, nicknamed the Jackal, became a two-weight World Champion by defeating Leo Santa Cruz in 2016?

9. With which English county did Belfast born cricketer Paul Stirling win the County Championship in 2016?

10. Who did Dennis Taylor beat in the 1985 World Snooker Championship Final?

# Sprint Finish

**Describe these ten sporting words
and phrases to your team...**

1. Mountain biking

2. Headwind

3. Jürgen Klinsmann

4. Paddle

5. Davis Cup

6. Double dribble

7. Three Lions

8. Willie Carson

9. Monaco Grand Prix

10. Trophy

# Game 44 Answers

**One-Minute Round**

1. MCG; 2. 3 Events in a Triathlon; 3. Tennis; 4. Wayne Rooney; 5. 1998; 6. Nine;
7. Iceland; 8. Terrance COPPER, Tun TIN, Arielle GOLD

**Mystery Guest**

Michael Schumacher, Rafael Nadal

**Home or Away**

1. Football. Marcus Rashford
2. Snooker. Ding Junhui

1. Athletics. Marathon
2. Boxing. George Groves

1. Cricket. Steve Smith
2. Rugby League. Leeds Rhinos

1. Tennis. Spain
2. Motor Racing. W Series

**Top Ten**

Athletics
Swimming
Wrestling
Shooting
Boxing
Diving
Gymnastics
Rowing
Basketball
Tennis

**Buzzer Round**

1. Jonathan Rea; 2. Ulster; 3. Pommel horse; 4. Mary Peters; 5. 2010; 6. Royal
Portrush; 7. Wales; 8. Carl Frampton; 9. Middlesex; 10. Steve Davis

# Game 45

# One-Minute Round

1. Which venue has hosted the World Snooker Championship since 1977?

2. Can you solve this sporting equation? '6P on a ST'

3. Which famous race begins with the Grand Depart?

4. 'REFERRED OGRE' is an anagram of which Grand Slam champion?

5. In which year did Adam Scott win the US Masters?

6. Over how many metres are all Olympic rowing races?

7. Y.E. Yang and Son Heung-min have both represented which country?

8. These three sports stars all share parts of their names with food you might find in a tin…

    Tamer **?** (Football)
    Andy **?** (Golf)
    **?** Campbell (Baseball)

# Mystery Guest

**In this round you are given three clues
to a sports star's identity.**

### Who is this Mystery Guest?

1. I was born in Alabama in 1961.

2. At the World Championships in 1991, I was part of an iconic battle with my compatriot Mike Powell.

3. I have won nine Olympic gold medals in total.

### Who is this Mystery Guest?

1. I won the Ballon d'Or three times in the 1970s.

2. I played football around the world but started and ended my career playing for Dutch teams.

3. I had my own signature move named after me.

# Home or Away

**In this round there is a choice of a home question for one point or an away question for two.**

*Do you want a home question on Rugby Union for one point or an away question on the Olympics for two?*

1. **Rugby Union.** Which 1991 World Cup winner is the top points scorer in internationals for Australia?

2. **The Olympics.** In 2008, Sarah Stevenson won Great Britain's first ever Olympic medal in which martial arts?

*Do you want a home question on Athletics for one point or an away question on Horse Racing for two?*

1. **Athletics.** In 1984, who became only the second person to ever successfully defend their Olympic decathlon title?

2. **Horse Racing.** Which racecourse hosts the longest and oldest of the English Classics, the St Leger Stakes?

*Do you want a home question on Cricket for one point or an away question on Ice Hockey for two?*

1. **Cricket.** Between 2008 and 2013, which spinner took 255 wickets for England in his 60 Tests?

2. **Ice Hockey.** Which NHL Ice Hockey team's franchise name comes first alphabetically?

*Do you want a home question on Football for one point or an away question on Cycling for two?*

1. **Football.** England and which other country are the two sides to have won in their only FIFA World Cup Final appearance?

2. **Cycling.** Laura Kenny has won double Olympic gold in the Team Pursuit and in which individual event?

# Top Ten

**Name the ten European winners of the
Open Championship between 1980 and 2020.**

There's a point for each one you correctly identify, but guess one
wrong and you lose your points from this round...

1 .................................................................

2 .................................................................

3 .................................................................

4 .................................................................

5 .................................................................

6 .................................................................

7 .................................................................

8 .................................................................

9 .................................................................

10 ................................................................

# Buzzer Round

**All the questions in this round all have a family connection...**

1. Which of the Williams' sisters won the Wimbledon Singles title first?

2. Father and son Chris and Stuart Broad have both played first-class cricket for which county?

3. Gary and Phil Neville's sister Tracey coached England to Commonwealth gold in which sport?

4. Manu Tuilagi plays rugby internationally for England, but for which Pacific Island nation have his five brothers played?

5. Husband and wife pairing Chris and Gabby Adcock have been European Champions in which sport?

6. In which did year Alistair and Jonny Brownlee first win Olympic medals in Triathlon?

7. Sean and Matty Longstaff both played football for which Premier League team in 2019?

8. Liverpudlian brothers Callum, Stephen, Liam and Paul Smith have all fought for world titles in which sport?

9. What is the surname of Olympic gold-winning hockey couple Kate and Helen?

10. What is the surname of the father and son drivers that won their Formula One world titles in 1982 and 2016 respectively?

# Sprint Finish

**Describe these ten sporting words
and phrases to your team...**

1. Steering wheel

2. Miami heat

3. Henman Hill

4. 180

5. Belly putter

6. Steven Gerrard

7. Blood replacement

8. Stump

9. Polo

10. Turnover

# Game 45 Answers

**One-Minute Round**
1. The Crucible; 2. 6 Pockets on a Snooker Table; 3. Tour de France; 4. Roger Federer; 5. 2013; 6. 2000m; 7. South Korea; 8. Tamer TUNA, Andy BEAN, SOUP Campbell

**Mystery Guest**
Carl Lewis, Johan Cruyff

**Home or Away**
1. Rugby Union. Michael Lynagh
2. The Olympics. Taekwondo

1. Athletics. Daley Thompson
2. Horse Racing. Doncaster

1. Cricket. Graeme Swann
2. Ice Hockey. Colorado Avalanche

1. Football. Spain
2. Cycling. Omnium

**Top Ten**
Seve Ballesteros
Sandy Lyle
Nick Faldo
Paul Lawrie
Padraig Harrington
Darren Clarke
Rory McIlroy
Henrik Stenson
Francesco Molinari
Shane Lowry

**Buzzer Round**
1. Venus; 2. Nottinghamshire; 3. Netball; 4. Samoa; 5. Badminton; 6. 2012;
7. Newcastle United; 8. Boxing; 9. Richardson-Walsh; 10. Rosberg (Keke and Nico)

# Game 46

# One-Minute Round

1. At which racecourse is the Irish Grand National held?

2. Can you solve this sporting equation? '50P for a B in D'

3. In which sport might you perform an Eskimo roll?

4. 'LEGGY BUREAU' is an anagram of which sport?

5. In which year did Diego Maradona famously score the 'Hand of God' goal?

6. How many minutes are there in a game of Basketball in the NBA?

7. Jarno Trulli and Fabio Fognini have both represented which country?

8. These three sports stars all share parts of their names with people you might associate with Camelot…

   Alex **?** (Boxing)
   **?** Kopp (Baseball)
   **?** Royle (Athletics)

# Mystery Guest

**In this round you are given three clues
to a sports star's identity.**

### Who is this Mystery Guest?

1. I am a former golfer, born in 1940 in Columbus, Ohio.

2. My company has designed over 400 golf courses around the world.

3. As of 2020, I have won the most major golf championships in history.

### Who is this Mystery Guest?

1. I have an older brother who competes in the same sport as me.

2. I am a former World Heavyweight Champion.

3. In my final fight in 2017, I was beaten by Anthony Joshua.

# Home or Away

**In this round there is a choice of a home question
for one point or an away question for two.**

*Do you want a home question on Athletics for one point or an
away question on Formula One for two?*

1. **Athletics.** Which six-time Paralympic champion won his eighth
   London Marathon in 2018?

2. **Formula One.** In 2013, who became only the third driver to win
   the Formula One World Championship four years in a row?

*Do you want a home question on Football for one point or an
away question on the Winter Olympics for two?*

1. **Football.** Between 2010 and 2020, which team won the League Cup
   on five occasions?

2. **Winter Olympics.** Which Winter Olympic sport sees competitors
   take part in cross-country skiing and rifle shooting?

*Do you want a home question on Tennis for one point or an away question on Fencing for two?*

1. **Tennis.** Which US Open champion reached three Wimbledon singles finals in the 2000s, losing to Roger Federer on each occasion?

2. **Fencing.** Which European country has won the most gold medals at the Olympics in Fencing?

*Do you want a home question on Golf for one point or an away question on Boxing for two?*

1. **Golf.** Which Spanish golfer won the European Tour Race to Dubai in 2019, a year after making a winning debut at the Ryder Cup?

2. **Boxing.** At the 2016 Olympics, what was the lightest weight of the boxing competition?

# Top Ten

**Name the top ten countries in the medal table at the 2018 Commonwealth Games.**

There's a point for each one you correctly identify, but guess one wrong and you lose your points from this round…

1 .................................................................

2 .................................................................

3 .................................................................

4 .................................................................

5 .................................................................

6 .................................................................

7 .................................................................

8 .................................................................

9 .................................................................

10 ................................................................

# Buzzer Round

**The answers to all the questions in this round begin with the letter T. In the case of a person it's the surname that will begin with that letter...**

1. Which Englishman won the 2019 World Snooker Championship?

2. At which football ground do Burnley play their home games?

3. Nicolás Massú and Fernando González have won Olympic medals for Chile in which sport?

4. Which country has won 29 Wrestling gold medals at the Olympics, their most successful sport at the games?

5. In 1964, who became the first bowler to take 300 Test wickets for England?

6. What is the franchise name of the NBA team based in Oklahoma City?

7. On which course did golfer Stewart Cink win the 2009 Open Championship?

8. Who scored Australia's only try in the 2003 Rugby Union World Cup Final?

9. In a multi-length race, what name is given to the move swimmers perform at the end of a length?

10. With which constructor did Jackie Stewart win two of his three Formula One World Championships?

# Sprint Finish

**Describe these ten sporting words
and phrases to your team...**

1.  Heavyweight

2.  Victory lap

3.  Foot fault

4.  King of the Mountains

5.  Helen Glover

6.  Goal line clearance

7.  The Magpies

8.  Bogey

9.  David Coleman

10. Half-pipe

# **Game 46** Answers

## One-Minute Round

1. Fairyhouse; 2. 50 Points for a Bullseye in Darts; 3. Kayaking; 4. Rugby League;
5. 1986; 6. 48; 7. Italy; 8 . Alex ARTHUR, MERLIN Kopp, LANCELOT Royle

## Mystery Guest

Jack Nicklaus, Wladimir Klitschko

## Home or Away

1. Athletics. David Weir
2. Formula One. Sebastian Vettel

1. Football. Manchester City
2. Winter Olympics. Biathlon

1. Tennis. Andy Roddick
2. Fencing. Italy

1. Golf. Jon Rahm
2. Boxing. Light flyweight

## Top Ten

Australia
England
India
Canada
New Zealand
South Africa
Wales
Scotland
Nigeria
Cyprus

## Buzzer Round

1. Judd Trump; 2. Turf Moor; 3. Tennis; 4. Turkey; 5. Fred Trueman; 6. Thunder;
7. Turnberry; 8. Lote Tuqiri; 9. Tumble turn; 10. Tyrrell

# Game 47

# One-Minute Round

1. The Circuit de la Sarthe in France hosts which motor race each year?

2. Can you solve this sporting equation? '2M and 2W in a MDTM'

3. Which race is associated with Valentine's and Foinavon?

4. 'QUEER SAINT' is an anagram of which Olympic sport?

5. In which year did Niki Lauda win the first of his three World Championships?

6. What position did Great Britain finish on the medal table at the Rio Olympics?

7. Grigor Dimitrov and Hristo Stoichkov have both represented which country?

8. These three sports stars all share parts of their names with things you might fry…

   **?** Hooper (Tennis)
   Mark **?** (Football)
   Oscar **?** (Cycling)

# Mystery Guest

**In this round you are given three clues
to a sports star's identity.**

### Who is this Mystery Guest?

1.  The only Grand Slam singles title I failed to win in my career was
    the French Open.

2.  I last reached world number one in 2000, a position I'd held for an
    accumulative total of 286 weeks in my career.

3.  I was well known for my grass court prowess, and had a 31-match
    winning streak at Wimbledon.

### Who is this Mystery Guest?

1.  My father was a two-time World Champion in a sport that I also
    made my name.

2.  I won the BBC Sports Personality of the Year award twice in
    the 1990s.

3.  I won the 1996 Formula One World Championship.

# Home or Away

**In this round there is a choice of a home question
for one point or an away question for two.**

*Do you want a home question on Football for one point or an
away question on Boxing for two?*

1. **Football.** Which European country has appeared in the World Cup
   Final on three occasions without winning the trophy?

2. **Boxing.** Which British boxer holds the record for the longest
   reigning super middleweight world champion?

*Do you want a home question on Cricket for one point or an away
question on American Football for two?*

1. **Cricket.** Which bowler took over 40 Ashes wickets against England
   in both 1981 and 1989?

2. **American Football.** Who are the only team to win the Super Bowl
   with a perfect record of winning every game in the season?

*Do you want a home question on Athletics for one point or an away question on Horse Racing for two?*

1. **Athletics.** Since 1997, who is the only sprinter to win the men's 100m at the World Championships that did not represent the USA or Jamaica?

2. **Horse Racing.** Which racecourse hosts the Welsh Grand National each year?

*Do you want a home question on Tennis for one point or an away question on the Winter Olympics for two?*

1. **Tennis.** Who, in 2019, lost a second successive Grand Slam final at the French Open, and later that year made the final of the season-ending ATP event for the first time?

2. **Winter Olympics.** In 2018, who became the only British person to win a second Winter Olympic gold medal, doing so in the Skeleton?

# Top Ten

**Name the ten Tier 1 Rugby Union players
that have scored the most points in
Internationals as of April 2020.**

There's a point for each one you correctly identify, but guess one
wrong and you lose your points from this round...

1 ............................................................

2 ............................................................

3 ............................................................

4 ............................................................

5 ............................................................

6 ............................................................

7 ............................................................

8 ............................................................

9 ............................................................

10 ............................................................

# Buzzer Round

**All the questions in this round are about Africa
and sports stars from that continent...**

1. Which African nation played in every Rugby Union World Cup
   between 1999 and 2019 but failed to win a match in that time?

2. From which club did Manchester City sign Ivorian midfielder Yaya
   Touré in 2010?

3. Heath Streak, Brendan Taylor and Murray Goodwin all played
   international cricket for which country?

4. Which South African golfer won the US Open twice in the 2000s?

5. At the 2018 Winter Olympics, former track and field star Simidele
   Adeagbo was Africa's first woman to compete in which sport?

6. Which Kenyan athlete won gold medals in the 800m at both the
   2012 and 2016 Olympics?

7. Who did Muhammad Ali defeat in the 'Rumble in the Jungle'
   in Zaire?

8. How many African nations played in the 2019 Netball World Cup?

9. Which country has won the African Cup of Nations football
   tournament a record number of times?

10. Which Zimbabwean swimmer won seven Olympic medals in the
    2000s, including two golds?

# Sprint Finish

**Describe these ten sporting words
and phrases to your team...**

1. Victoria Pendleton

2. Relay

3. Double fault

4. London Irish

5. Boxing gloves

6. John Parrott

7. Brands Hatch

8. Tumble turn

9. 1500m

10. Lionesses

# Game 47 Answers

**One-Minute Round**

1. 24 Hours of Le Mans; 2. 2 Men and 2 Women in a Mixed Doubles Tennis Match; 3. Grand National; 4. Equestrian; 5. 1975; 6. Second; 7. Bulgaria; 8. CHIP Hooper, Mark FISH, Oscar EGG

**Mystery Guest**

Pete Sampras, Damon Hill

**Home or Away**

1. Football. Netherlands
2. Boxing. Joe Calzaghe

1. Cricket. Terry Alderman
2. American Football. Miami Dolphins

1. Athletics. Kim Collins
2. Horse Racing. Chepstow

1. Tennis. Dominic Thiem
2. Winter Olympics. Lizzy Yarnold

**Top Ten**

Dan Carter
Jonny Wilkinson
Neil Jenkins
Ronan O'Gara
Diego Domínguez
Stephen Jones
Andrew Mehrtens
Owen Farrell
Michael Lynagh
Percy Montgomery

**Buzzer Round**

1. Namibia; 2. Barcelona; 3. Zimbabwe; 4. Retief Goosen; 5. Skeleton; 6. David Rudisha; 7. George Foreman; 8. Four; 9. Egypt; 10. Kirsty Coventry

# Game 48

# One-Minute Round

1. Which Spanish team play their home games at the Wanda Metropolitano?

2. Can you solve this sporting equation? '6OGM for CH'

3. The DFB-Pokal Cup is the domestic cup football competition in which European country?

4. 'TALL KEBABS' is an anagram of which sport?

5. In which year did Phil Taylor win his first World Darts Championship?

6. How many courts are used for matches during the Wimbledon Championships?

7. Umar Gul and Shahid Afridi have both played Test cricket for which country?

8. These three sports stars all share parts of their names with places that you might live…

   Carolyn **?** (Swimming)
   David **?** (Football)
   Rachael **?** (Figure Skating)

# Mystery Guest

**In this round you are given three clues
to a sports star's identity.**

### Who is this Mystery Guest?

1.  I won a silver medal on the water at the Atlanta Olympics.

2.  In 2013, I won the America's Cup.

3.  I have won four gold medals and am Great Britain's most successful
    Olympic sailor.

### Who is this Mystery Guest?

1.  In 1995, my dad became my coach.

2.  I won gold for the USA at the 2000 Olympics.

3.  I lost to my sister three times in the final of Wimbledon.

# Home or Away

**In this round there is a choice of a home question for one point or an away question for two.**

*Do you want a home question on Football for one point or an away question on Snooker for two?*

1. **Football.** Wayne Rooney is England's record goal scorer with 53 goals, but whose record did he break in September 2015?

2. **Snooker.** Who won the 2020 Masters, five years after becoming World Snooker Champion for the first time?

*Do you want a home question on Rugby Union for one point or an away question on Rowing for two?*

1. **Rugby Union.** In 2011, against England, which Irishman broke the record for the most tries in the Six Nations when he scored his 25th try?

2. **Rowing.** Rebecca Romero became the first British woman to win Olympic medals in two different summer sports by adding to the rowing silver she won in Athens with a gold in which event?

*Do you want a home question on Cricket for one point or an away question on American Football for two?*

1. **Cricket.** Which country has reached four Cricket World Cup semi-finals without ever playing in the final?

2. **American Football.** In 2019, which quarterback broke Peyton Manning's NFL record for career touchdown passes?

*Do you want a home question on Athletics for one point or an away question on the Winter Olympics for two?*

1. **Athletics.** Who won 107 consecutive finals in the 400m hurdles between 1977 and 1987, including the Olympic final on his home soil in 1984?

2. **Winter Olympics.** What curling event was added to the Winter Olympic programme for the 2018 Games in PyeongChang?

# Top Ten

**Name the ten football teams that have played the most games in the Champions League as of the end of the 2019–20 season.**

There's a point for each one you correctly identify, but guess one wrong and you lose your points from this round...

1 ...................................................................

2 ...................................................................

3 ...................................................................

4 ...................................................................

5 ...................................................................

6 ...................................................................

7 ...................................................................

8 ...................................................................

9 ...................................................................

10 ...................................................................

# Buzzer Round

**The answers to all the questions in this round begin with the letter N. In the case of a person it's the surname that will begin with that letter...**

1. Which country topped the medal table at the 2018 Winter Olympics?

2. Which golfer won the last of his 18 majors in 1986?

3. Which Rugby Union team play their home games at Franklin's Gardens?

4. Which tennis player won the 1998 Wimbledon Ladies' Singles title?

5. How is a perfect leg of darts better known?

6. Which country lost both the 2015 and 2019 Cricket World Cup finals?

7. In which sport have Team Bath and Manchester Thunder won Superleague titles?

8. Which football team won the European Cup Final in 1979 and 1980?

9. What is the franchise name of the NBA basketball team based in Denver?

10. Marianne Vos is an Olympic and World cycling champion from which country?

# Sprint Finish

**Describe these ten sporting words
and phrases to your team...**

1. Baggy green

2. Floor

3. Bill Beaumont

4. One-two

5. Becher's Brook

6. Hawkeye

7. Quiver

8. Darren Clarke

9. Red card

10. Back spin

# Game **48** Answers

**One-Minute Round**
1. Atlético Madrid; 2. 6 Olympic Gold Medals for Chris Hoy; 3. Germany;
4. Basketball; 5. 1990; 6. 18; 7. Pakistan; 8. Carolyn HOUSE, David VILLA,
Rachael FLAT

**Mystery Guest**
Ben Ainslie, Venus Williams

**Home or Away**
1.   Football. Bobby Charlton
2.   Snooker. Stuart Bingham

1.   Rugby Union. Brian O'Driscoll
2.   Rowing. Cycling

1.   Cricket. South Africa
2.   American Football. Drew Brees

1.   Athletics. Ed Moses
2.   Winter Olympics. Mixed Doubles

**Top Ten**
Real Madrid
Bayern Munich
Barcelona
Manchester United
Juventus
AC Milan
Liverpool
Benfica
Porto
Ajax

**Buzzer Round**
1. Norway; 2. Jack Nicklaus; 3. Northampton Saints; 4. Jana Novotná;
5. Nine-dart finish; 6. New Zealand; 7. Netball; 8. Nottingham Forest; 9. Nuggets;
10. Netherlands

# Game 49

# One-Minute Round

1.  Where do Worcester play their Rugby Union home games?

2.  Can you solve this sporting equation? '68PP for MS in FO'

3.  The UK Championship, the World Championship and which other tournament make up snooker's Triple Crown?

4.  'REPAY CATCALLS' is an anagram of which football team?

5.  In which year did Linford Christie become Olympic champion?

6.  How many stages are in the Tour de France?

7.  Katie Archibald and Grace Reid have both won Commonwealth gold for which country?

8.  These three sports stars all share parts of their names with American states...

    **?** Hall (Golf)
    **?** Vassilev (Football)
    Joe **?** (American Football)

# Mystery Guest

**In this round you are given three clues
to a sports star's identity.**

### Who is this Mystery Guest?

1. At 13 years old, I won two gold medals for Team GB at the Paralympic Games in Beijing.

2. In 2008, I was named BBC Young Sports Personality of the Year.

3. Four years later, in London, I beat the World Record for the 400m Freestyle by five seconds.

### Who is this Mystery Guest?

1. I was best known for playing for the Edmonton Oilers and the LA Kings.

2. I am the only NHL player to score over 200 points in a season.

3. I am famous for wearing the number 99 on my jersey.

# Home or Away

**In this round there is a choice of a home question
for one point or an away question for two.**

*Do you want a home question on Cricket for one point or an away
question on Formula One for two?*

1.  **Cricket.** Which West Indian scored over 8,000 runs and took
    more than 200 wickets during a Test career spanning the 1950s,
    1960s and 1970s?

2.  **Formula One.** As of 2020, which German driver held the record
    for most races in Formula One without finishing on the podium?

*Do you want a home question on Football for one point or an
away question on Swimming for two?*

1.  **Football.** In 1967, who became the first British club to win the
    European Cup with that team going on to be nicknamed the
    Lisbon Lions?

2.  **Swimming.** Between 2010 and 2014, which South African
    swimmer won 200m Butterfly gold at the Olympics, the World
    Championships and the Commonwealth Games?

*Do you want a home question on Golf for one point or an away question on Darts for two?*

1. **Golf.** Which golfer won his first major, the 2011 US Open, by a tournament record eight strokes, and in the following three years, won three more majors?

2. **Darts.** As of 2020, which Englishman is the only player to win the Premier League Darts that hasn't won the World Championship?

*Do you want a home question on Rugby Union for one point or an away question on Basketball for two?*

1. **Rugby Union.** Who became the first man to lead the All Blacks in two World Cup Final victories?

2. **Basketball.** Since 1992, which is the only country other than the USA to win the men's basketball gold at the Summer Olympics?

# Top Ten

**Name the ten men that topped the tennis
World Rankings between 1975 and 1995.**

There's a point for each one you correctly identify, but guess one
wrong and you lose your points from this round...

1  ..............................................................................

2  ..............................................................................

3  ..............................................................................

4  ..............................................................................

5  ..............................................................................

6  ..............................................................................

7  ..............................................................................

8  ..............................................................................

9  ..............................................................................

10  ..............................................................................

# Buzzer Round

**All the questions in this round are about Wales
and sports stars from that country...**

1. Which country did Wales beat 3-1 to reach the semi-finals of
   Euro 2016?

2. In which sport have the Cardiff Devils been National champions?

3. Which forward became Wales's most capped Rugby Union player
   in 2019?

4. In which city did swimmer Jazz Carlin win two Olympic silver
   medals?

5. Which Welsh cyclist won the Tour de France in 2018?

6. In which sport have Mark Webster, Gerwyn Price and Richie
   Burnett all competed at the World Championships?

7. Which Welshman won the Sports Personality of the Year award
   in 2009?

8. In which city did Tanni Grey-Thompson win the last of her 11
   Paralympic gold medals?

9. Nathan Cleverly is a two-time World Champion in which sport?

10. Which Welshman reached two World Snooker Championship Finals
    in the 2000s, losing both of them?

# Sprint Finish

**Describe these ten sporting words and phrases to your team...**

1. Bolero

2. Coxless four

3. Sydney Swans

4. Gareth Southgate

5. Routine

6. Flop shot

7. Dina Asher-Smith

8. Royal box

9. Man of steel

10. Bicycle kick

# Game 49 Answers

**One-Minute Round**
1. Sixways; 2. 68 Pole Positions for Michael Schumacher in Formula One;
3. The Masters; 4. Crystal Palace; 5. 1992; 6. 21; 7. Scotland; 8. GEORGIA Hall,
INDIANA Vassilev, Joe MONTANA

**Mystery Guest**
Ellie Simmonds, Wayne Gretzky

**Home or Away**
1. Cricket. Garry Sobers
2. Formula One. Nico Hülkenberg

1. Football. Celtic
2. Swimming. Chad le Clos

1. Golf. Rory McIlroy
2. Darts. James Wade

1. Rugby Union. Richie McCaw
2. Basketball. Argentina

**Top Ten**
Jimmy Connors
Bjørn Borg
John McEnroe
Ivan Lendl
Mats Wilander
Stefan Edberg
Boris Becker
Jim Courier
Pete Sampras
Andre Agassi

**Buzzer Round**
1. Belgium; 2. Ice hockey; 3. Alun Wyn Jones; 4. Rio de Janeiro; 5. Geraint
Thomas; 6. Darts; 7. Ryan Giggs; 8. Athens; 9. Boxing; 10. Matthew Stevens

# Game 50

# One-Minute Round

1. Which venue hosted the BDO World Darts Championship between 1986 and 2019?

2. Can you solve this sporting equation? '1WOGM for JT and CD'

3. Which British race track features the corners Becketts and Luffield?

4. 'WRITES GOOD' is an anagram of which major champion?

5. In which year did Virginia Wade win the Wimbledon Ladies' Singles title?

6. How many international centuries did Sachin Tendulkar score in his career?

7. Morgan Parra and Teddy Thomas have both played international rugby for which country?

8. These three sports stars all share parts of their names with people you might find in a hospital...

   Trevor **?** (Darts)
   Mary **?** (Speed Skating)
   Tiffany **?** (Athletics)

# Mystery Guest

**In this round you are given three clues
to a sports star's identity.**

### *Who is this Mystery Guest?*

1.  I made my Premier League debut in 1998.

2.  I captained my country at the World Cup in 2010 and 2014.

3.  I scored as my team won the 2005 Champions League Final.

### *Who is this Mystery Guest?*

1.  I have written a children's book series about an elite training school for young athletes.

2.  I have won four Olympic medals, including 400m Gold in Beijing.

3.  I am the first British woman to win two World Athletics Championship gold medals.

# Home or Away

**In this round there is a choice of a home question for one point or an away question for two.**

*Do you want a home question on Tennis for one point or an away question on the Olympics for two?*

1.  **Tennis.** Which Australian tennis player won his only Wimbledon singles title in 2002 by beating David Nalbandian in the final?

2.  **The Olympics.** In which sport did Peter Wilson become only the second person to win gold for Great Britain since 1990?

*Do you want a home question on Rugby Union for one point or an away question on Horse Racing for two?*

1.  **Rugby Union.** In 1999, which country won the last ever Five Nations, with Alan Tait scoring five tries in the tournament?

2.  **Horse Racing.** In March 2019, Bryony Frost became the first woman to win a Grade One horse race by winning the Ryanair Chase on which racecourse?

*Do you want a home question on Football for one point or an away question on Snooker for two?*

1. **Football.** In November 2019, which English striker became the fastest player to reach 20 Champions League goals, surpassing the previous record set by Alessandro Del Piero?

2. **Snooker.** Who won six World Championships in the 1970s and was the first player to top snooker's world rankings?

*Do you want a home question on Golf for one point or an away question on the Winter Olympics for two?*

1. **Golf.** Between 2000 and 2020, only Davis Love III and which other golfer have captained the USA to victory in the Ryder Cup?

2. **Winter Olympics.** Who is the only skater to win a medal for Great Britain in Short Track Speed Skating, doing so in 1994?

# Top Ten

**Name the ten countries that have played the
most games at the men's Cricket World Cups.**

There's a point for each one you correctly identify, but guess one
wrong and you lose your points from this round...

1 ...........................................................................

2 ...........................................................................

3 ...........................................................................

4 ...........................................................................

5 ...........................................................................

6 ...........................................................................

7 ...........................................................................

8 ...........................................................................

9 ...........................................................................

10 ...........................................................................

# Buzzer Round

**All the questions in this round are about the
2000 Summer Olympics in Sydney...**

1. Which Australian was the most successful swimmer at the Sydney Olympics?

2. Rower Steve Redgrave won the Olympic title in the coxless fours in Sydney, bringing his career gold medal total to how many?

3. Which Australian won 400m gold on the track at her home Olympics?

4. Which multi-sport event was first introduced to the Olympic programme in 2000?

5. With which African country did Samuel Eto'o win men's football gold as a 19-year-old?

6. In which sport was the only gold medal contested between the USA and Cuba?

7. Which American tennis player won gold medals in the women's singles and women's doubles?

8. Which British boxer won gold at Super-Heavyweight in 2000?

9. Which sport took place in Sydney Harbour?

10. In which event did Jason Queally win Great Britain's only cycling gold of the Games?

# Sprint Finish

**Describe these ten sporting words
and phrases to your team...**

1. Sale Sharks

2. Perfect ten

3. Bird's nest

4. Ryder Cup

5. Velodrome

6. Ryan Giggs

7. LBW

8. Glass jaw

9. Fumble

10. Slipstream